A
THOUSAND
FLYING
THINGS

A NOVEL

KATHRYN BROWN RAMSPERGER

Relax. Read. Repeat.

A THOUSAND FLYING THINGS
By Kathryn Brown Ramsperger
Published by TouchPoint Press
Brookland, AR 72417
www.touchpointpress.com

Softcover ISBN: 978-1-956851-64-9

Editor: Kimberly Coghlan
Cover Design: Estella Vukovic

First Edition

Printed in the United States of America.

Better a bird in the hand than a thousand flying things.
—Sudanese proverb

*The oak tree
And the cypress
Grow not in each other's shadows.*
—Khalil Gibran

To my children
Sean Dylan and Aimee Xiao Wei
Who taught me
Most of what I know
About the world.

We run from love

Though it is what we most want.

Seldom do we gain the wisdom it shares.

Rarely does love find us again.

Never do we see it coming.

Or how.

CHAPTER ONE:
FAIR PLAY

February 14, 1991
Piecewood Displaced Persons Camp
Near Bor, Southern Sudan

Dianna peeks through the smooth, worn canvas flap of her thatched hut. It's only 30 days since she arrived. It might as well be 300. She pulls on a T-shirt and shorts for her daily run before the heat sets in. She runs no matter where she is. Here, the children, already awake, follow her. It's a game to them. They'd never imagine her reason for it.

She began running to maintain weight. Then, she ran to forget her past. Now, she runs to avoid thinking about her future. The endorphin rush is better than food, much better than romance. It's a multi-purpose tool for boredom, anxiety, strategizing, or blotting out thought.

These children mean everything to her because her presence in Africa is what she has left. She has a year to reach them. A year from now, most will join the fighting, or the dead. Reaching even one would be enough reward for the time spent in this restless, ragged heat. Reaching a few would be a miracle. Books are her only tool.

Her eye catches a motion in her peripheral vision. At first, she jumps. It's a crouching animal, a hyena, or worse. But no, it's a tiny boy, no more than five. She's about to stop and ask him why he's here, but he disappears into the predawn shadows. She keeps running, but she asks another boy who he is.

"Khalil," the boy answers with a shrug.

"Why is Khalil here?"

"He is with Commander Biel." She doesn't like the sound of that. What warring tribal leader would bring a family member? He must have kidnapped him, or worse, bought him. She'll have to tell her colleagues, especially the social worker, Mirembe, when they visit next month. But she's not sure who she can trust. Most of her colleagues are five or more kilometers away, not that she minds. The U.N. has a new policy to enlist regional staff for its programs. "Teach a man to fish," and all that. She can't trust any of them—or anyone in the bush—white or Black, Muslim or Tribal, Arab or Dinka, aid worker or resident—until they prove their trustworthiness. That usually means divulging their allegiance in this layered war. It's useless hoping to make friends here.

She's certain now that her teaching is a diversion, that less than a kilometer away, these boys are being prepared to shoot rifles, even missiles. Biel is training them for his war and pretending to teach them to read. Yet perhaps she can save one or two lives.

She must be careful how she presents it to the woman called

Mirembe at the delegation. Without Biel's approval of her mission here at camp, Dianna will be sent home. The government wants her here, but Biel, he's forced to let her teach to receive U.N. aid. She suspects he's using her as a ruse for more international funding. A shiver courses down her back with drops of sweat.

That afternoon, the boys straggle into the schoolroom, their mouths curving up when they see her, their dark eyes bright, their fingertips reaching into her pockets, searching for Life Savers or cigarettes she brought to make friends. They speak to her with their eyes instead of their mouths. Her suitcase full of bribes—piles of unboxed Marlboros—is almost empty. Her supposed students turn up their noses at anything, like a pencil, that they cannot inhale with their lungs or bellies.

They are still a bit young to be sticking needles in their arms, but that too will come, once they see some action. She's observed the dull eyes of teenaged soldiers-in-training too many times to imagine these bright-eyed boys' futures would turn out otherwise. Young combatants are a tradition and necessity here. Sudan has had conflict, usually civil war, since the late 1950s, when the country claimed independence from Britain and Egypt. They've been fighting here as long as she's been alive. The boy soldiers, only slightly older than the students, are starving for food but laden with pharmaceuticals. They march through wasted grassland covering oceans of untapped petroleum. All their fighting will never yield a drop for them.

As she waits to begin, Dianna takes out an emery board, a vestige of home. Her nails are crooked and cracked from the heat, drawing water, and chopping weeds from around the doorway to her hut.

Funny how its rough, sandy surface, which echoes this world but also reminds her of home, comforts her. Right, left, right, left, she files down the nails until she reaches the skin where the nail ends and the finger begins.

She is filing when more children skip in, brandishing a knife, a rusty fishing hook, or a spent grenade.

"What?" an almost-adolescent boy asks, peering at the strange stick in her folded hands. It's the first time she's seen him.

Time and again, Dianna has explained. Time and again, the children fail to understand. "It's a tool for my fingernails," she tells him.

"Need?" he asks, shaking his head, either mystified or judgmental. The children may learn to read before they learn the use of a manicure utensil. Yet still, she files. It is her statement of faith.

Some boys don't ever show. Dianna watches them performing their chores, eating their stewy, beany fu, preparing for nightfall, marching in formation. Still, these rations are infinitely better than the boiled leaves and grass they had before. They never meet her eye, and she knows not to push. They come to her only if their curiosity to learn overtakes their fear of their tribal leader Daniel Biel's disapproval. These children owe everything, including their survival, to him.

She's been on the receiving end of Biel's judgment and wouldn't want to be in the path of his anger. It arrives without warning like a snake coiled under the brush. He's not happy she's here. The government forced this relationship, probably to meet some sort of educational quota. Countries with abuses of human rights and low literacy rates don't receive much international aid. He wants money to fund the military he's building that's full of children, and he's getting it by calling his training ground a language school. She's little more than a babysitter.

Biel's a funny one. She can't figure him out entirely. She's seen him take time with each boy, ensuring they have enough to eat, that they are groomed, that they have moments of play in addition to work. He calls them his "little men." They worship him, and so they fear getting close to her.

She stretches, rolling her head to get out the kinks, rubs off the cold sweat, flicks away a minute, insistent insect. She wanders outside to see if anyone else is showing up and notices a flowering bush she can't remember being there yesterday. She strolls over to smell its perfume. Bending over the plant, she expects a jasmine blossom's gentle, white scent. Instead, thousands of swarming insects fly every which way. She backs up, shocked, trying to avoid them, batting them away from her face. What she thought were white petals are flapping wings that have eaten any bud that tried to appear. Things in the bush are never as simple as they appear. Impressions of people are even more deceptive. Like Biel. Maybe like Mirembe at the delegation, too. Even though she likes her, she can't trust her.

Today she's reading from *The Jungle Book*, but none of them are listening. The few boys in front of her are exhausted before the day begins from yesterday's hard work and training. They probably have little time in their day for fantasy stories with talking tigers and snakes. Nothing like their lives. Mowgli is Indian, and the story is implausible and sometimes racist. A colonialist wrote it over one hundred years ago.

She sees Thon sneer each time she reads the label "Man Cub." She should have thought to call him Mowgli throughout. Twenty years ago, when she was about Thon's age, Dianna fell in love with this novel because of its foreignness, its animals, and its message, but it's not what she should be reading aloud here.

"This book was written a very long time ago, and it's about a jungle, not Sudan," she explains, her gaze fixed upon Thon.

"Men are not animals," the boy answers, picking at his front tooth with a blade of grain.

She nods in agreement and puts down the book, but Alier protests. "I want to hear what happens to the boy!"

"Shhhhh!" The entire room shushes him and shames him. His head hangs down.

She looks around the room. "We call this story a fable. It's meant to have a message. It's not meant to be reality but to reflect reality. Shall I continue?" she asks no one in particular, least of all Alier, though he gives her a pleading glance.

Chol rests his chin on his hands, almost asleep. Jok's eyes wander around the room. Mabior comes up to her "desk," made of two crates, and tries to dig into her pocket a second time. She hears the first threads rip from cloth. There, he's ruined her jeans.

"Stop it!" Dianna hisses at him and almost slaps his hand but catches herself. He's just a child, and she can't afford to make enemies here. She catches his eye. He's laughing at her. She feels new sweat trickling down from her forehead to the wrinkled crow's foot that's getting deeper beside her left eye, to the nape of her neck to the bare part of her blistered shoulder. Abe, almost a teen, sucks on an unlit cigarette. She doesn't allow them to smoke in her presence, even though she's their dealer. At least she's kept that much under her control.

School is over for her as much as for them. They've been here almost an hour. She slams the book shut and drops it with a thud on her crates.

After class, the boys play football with an ancient, deflated soccer ball. They use tent poles as goal posts and the younger boys as goalies.

She brings her old Polaroid camera out. The boys drop their football and race toward this contraption, a camera from her past, but an object these boys have never seen. The resulting yellow, blurred images create quite a stir in this little camp. The children love to see themselves. They delight in making faces for the camera. They even primp sometimes, hoping she will choose to snap one of them. It is more than a conversation starter; it is a showstopper, marketing her words with their pictures.

She lets the boys roam around the pile of dusty photos and moves back to the shade of the canopied "schoolroom." Its stale air reminds her of her days in her North Carolina frame house, pre-air conditioning. As a girl, she lay in her four-poster, the air settling above her bed like a bubble too thick to prick. Moist but unyielding, it hovered as she lay in wait to leave that bedroom, that house, just as she is standing by to leave this place. She lets her thoughts unravel, barely noticing the boys at play.

She is hard pressed to determine which makes her feel emptier. This "schoolroom" is not much more than a tent. On rainy days, they must retreat to the tiny cinderblock closet of books, which is even more stifling. At least in North Carolina, she could visit the library. Books could make her forget the heavy air, the heat electrifying up her spine, her mother lying down in the next room, in her own sort of limbo. Books could even rid her of the pain of her monthly cycle or empty stomach when she was sent to her room without dinner. Reading's more important than running. Reading is more important than food. It fills the emptiness of this place when she longs for love and attention.

Yet would words ever mean as much to these boys as they did to Dianna? Would they lay down their rifles to turn the pages of the books she provided? Her mind pushes against the languid heat that presses her into the earth, and her lungs try to take in more air. The smell of overused cooking oil, reminiscent of the many meals fried in it, cuts the air like a scythe. She longs for just one ice cube. That is when she sees a young child's hand.

The hand waves at her from behind a large nearby rock. Flat on top, nature's idea of a throne, the stone hides the rest of the child's body. The hand itself, though, is a work of art. It is a hand a hyena could tear off with one swift chomp. Tiny, ragged fingernails, dirt caked over hidden fingerprints, flies buzzing this way and that. Yet the wrist is another thing altogether. Smooth and shiny and strong. She takes up her Polaroid and begins snapping. The shutter clicks, and the photos whirl out until the film is gone. They fall at her feet, creating a small dust storm. The specks float suspended in the air, then rest one by one on the photos.

She wants to wash his hands to see what lies beneath this grime, so she walks around the rock obscuring the body that owns this miniature man's hand. It's the boy from this morning.

"Hello?" She wonders if he will understand even that simple greeting.

"Hey," he answers.

Her eyes go wide. How does he know that word? Most boys know "hi" or "hello," but seldom use it because she greets them in their own language. And this boy looks barely old enough to speak many words at all.

"I teach myself book." The boy smiles. "You help?"

"Do you speak English?" Dianna fumbles in a mixture of English, Arabic, and Dinka.

"Engoish." The little boy smiles again, attempting to mimic her sounds. Then, he slaps her hand with his, reaches in her pocket, finds an English tea biscuit, and pops it whole into his mouth. "Tank."

Dianna laughs at the mispronunciation, wondering how long it took him to learn the sentence he greeted her with. Her heart is in her ears. She may have found her student.

"Name?" she asks.

"Annee," he answers.

She laughs again, this time a broad, imp-like Dianna laugh, a laugh she barely recollects.

"No, that's my name. I'm Dianna." Her fingers point to her chest, correcting him, showing him that this is how to pronounce her name. His beautiful, muddy palm slips around them. "You?" She points at his chest.

"Ka. Leel," he answers, sounding it out just as she did for him.

She does not know if both words form his name, whether it is a variation of some Nuer pronoun, or whether he has made it up himself.

"You mean this name?" She writes it out for him in the sand, and he nods. "How do you know my name?" she asks.

He doesn't understand the question. He simply stares at her with a certain fascination. Biel must have mentioned her to some of the boys. That was a good sign. He probably couldn't pronounce her last name, so he tried her first name just to mispronounce it.

He giggles, and his broad smile, still with its baby teeth, makes her want to hug him, but she doesn't. It is possible he was plucked from his village before he even answered to the name his mother called him. Many of these boys were orphans, and still, others were sent away, pawning, they called it. They were lent to others so that they—and the rest of the family—would not starve. The official word was that they were child laborers. Yet turning over this practice to reveal its dirty underside showed a far grimmer picture: slaves, sex slaves, child soldiers. Sacrifices, yet sacrifices with the hope of a fuller belly, and fuller for the conscripts than for their parents.

They walk hand in hand toward the canopy. They plop onto the ground, and he curls his elbow into her lap. Polaroid pictures look up at them through the earth like a faded carpet. Khalil picks up his image and squints. "Khalil?" he asks.

"Khalil." Dianna puts away her camera while smiling at his realization that he is the subject of the photograph. She chooses a book from a nearby stack, opens it to page one, and begins to read. As she mouths each word, he repeats it after her. He points at the detailed illustrations of leafy branches and curvy women in full skirts and stays. He points at the letters. Beatrix Potter's bunnies and hedgehogs dance in a land of cobras and hippos. He's interested in books! She wants to get to know him, help him succeed.

She has just broken a professional and personal credo—never get close to anyone again, especially not a client or student. She smiles in dazed but sated wonder. She always thought it would be a tall, dark man walking through camp who posed the most risk to her heart. And here, this little boy has grabbed it with one sentence and a few fingers. She will give him a good washing, make sure he is free from parasites, give him a T-shirt and a book all his own. Tomorrow, she will speak to Biel. This boy could not possibly be old enough for military training.

Khalil seems in awe of her classroom, the only one of its kind in the camp. He runs his hands over the wall and floor, and his deep-set, round eyes rove up and down again. People here at camp reside in thatched mud huts or sleep under flimsy tents. Many boys sleep in the open air. This "schoolhouse" has one cinderblock wall, though the other sides are open to the air. His delicate hands glide over each brick's cold, rough surface, one by one, as though it were a sculpture. If he even knows what a sculpture is. She fills a vat with all the cold water they can haul, pours soap into it, and orders him in. Khalil is having none of it. He is not getting his uniform wet. He crouches in the corner, still all smiles, but head wagging from side to side, "No." She hauls him in his strange uniform, which resembles ragged shorts and surgical scrubs more than fatigues, and dumps him into the vat. He couldn't weigh more than forty pounds, but he is arms and legs and sharp nails, flailing, no other sound. Then he is still as she pours the soapy water over him—and scrubs, scrubs his work-torn fingernails. He relaxes and blows bubbles. And gradually, the smooth, burnished skin shines through.

• • •

Biel stands outside his thatched domed abode, which serves as home, office, and covert military headquarters. He's smoking a cigar and tosses ash over his shoulder. He stiffens as he watches her approach, the lion preparing for battle. She leans forward in response.

"Dr. Biel, I wanted to express my thanks for the blanket. It was you who left it at my door?" She extends her hand. He does not take it. She bows instead, acknowledging the rebuff.

"Yes, it was I." He stares her down. She assumes he is waiting for the real reason she is here. The sun dips, barely a slip over the mountains in the distance.

"The boys are making progress." Dianna twists the cuff of her shirt with her fingers, around and around, like her mother used to twist her hair. Nerves.

"Yes?" He is not giving an inch.

"I—I want to ask you about this boy I have met." She looks at the dust on her feet, kicks it off only to find more dust.

"Yes?" He seems impatient to get on with his smoking. "What of it?"

"His name is Khalil."

"Khalil?" His expression has changed—malleable, fluid, and his lip twitches at one corner. He throws both shoulders back and steadies himself on a nearby fence post. "What do you want with Khalil?"

"He knows a few words of English. He has asked me to teach him to read." She gulps, pausing for his reaction.

The air is as silent as the static charge preceding a lightning bolt.

Biel grips the fence post, digs his feet into the dust as far as they will go, which is not far.

She tries again. "Dr. Biel, surely Khalil is too young to be in training. He can barely be more than seven!" She realizes her ironic use of the word "young," and she finds tears pricking the corners of her eyes.

"Khalil is too young to learn to read!" Biel's voice booms across the savannah.

"How old is he? He seems old enough to work for you."

"Neither his age nor reading ability should concern you!"

"He needs a teacher as much as any other boy in this camp."

He laughs out loud. This is the first laugh she has ever heard from him, and she does not like the sound of it. She backs away without bothering to keep up appearances.

He wags his finger in front of her face. "Khalil is mine, you hear me? Don't you hitch your high humanitarian hopes on my boy, you understand?"

Dianna is taken aback. Could he mean "son"? She cannot believe he would have his own son at this desolate place, even if it is home to him. And why would his son be here without his mother?

Biel's face closes in on hers, and she can smell the cigar, pungent and alarming. "If I ever see him under that canopy with you, you will never again be teaching anyone in my country," he says, enunciating each syllable, his pronunciation impeccable. His consonants click staccato against his teeth. The lisp she noticed during their first meeting is not apparent at all right now. How his enemies must cower in front of him! Her legs are shaking. She's pulled a button off her shirt cuff.

He turns and takes long leaps of steps toward his hut. He throws the cigar behind him. It lands at her feet.

●   ●   ●

How will she handle his threats? Her thoughts race back and forth like caged animals. Who can she report Biel's behavior to without it getting back to him? Who will believe her? She's all alone here. He could slit her throat and dump her; no one would know for weeks.

She stills her trembling hands and inhales. This might be her most challenging mission, but it's not her first. The best way of coping with stress is tidying. It steadies the mind. Some called that behavior OCD; she calls it sanity. With little to organize, Dianna busies herself stacking and restacking books, dusting them, only to watch the particles poise in a sunbeam, then resettle. She can't get rid of the dust any more than she can change Biel's mind. It's a puzzle, like the Chinese finger puzzles that trap you inside if you make the wrong move, where you push instead of pull to escape. She's used to tweaking her goals amid the nuanced politics and deep secrets in the developing world, but past obstacles pale next to Southern Sudan, and more so, to Biel. Is he truly the monster she sees him as?

She realizes she's holding her breath and breathes in again. With a decade of experience under her belt, she's up to it. She's spent a decade in Africa, mostly southern and eastern. Fed up with him, she'll do whatever it takes to ensure Khalil's safety.

She was born into a military family, spawned from farmers, her childhood carved up between military bases, small towns, and countryside. As a result, she pronounced the cold season "win-TER," with an accentuated "t," while her parents said, "WIN-tah," accenting the first syllable. They teased her about it, made her feel like she'd been born on Mars instead of the Midwest. Her grandparents barely said the word because they lived in the South but slurred the word when they did utter it. Her old love Qasim pronounced it "win-terh" with a rolled "r" in the back of his throat. She'd loved his "r's," his differences, and he loved hers, rather than judging them. He didn't bully her like her family, but even so, she'd never felt good enough for him. She believed he wanted to make her presentable to his friends and family, but now, she's not so sure he kept her away from them for that reason. He probably wanted to protect her from *them*.

He hadn't understood she didn't need protecting. Her father had PTSD—she knew that now, and her mother may have been bipolar before she declined into dementia. If she could survive her family and thrive, she could've handled Qasim's family. And she can survive Biel and Sudan. It's just like any other mission, just more isolated—and with more weapons.

As soon as she was eighteen, she'd run as far away as she could afford, first to college, then to a young writer, who synthesized her angst into creativity, then to Manhattan, where she'd met Qasim. He'd shaped her in a way her family could not. Yet love hadn't been enough for her. She'd felt trapped in expectation. Now she wonders if her loved ones expected change in her—or if she'd expected it in herself. She hadn't loved herself, and he'd not seemed to offer a future.

People who'd endured trauma were like that. Her, too. So, she'd run again to Africa, from them all. They'd only been lovers for a year.

Qasim never told his family about her. They probably would have disapproved of any relationship with her—a young, naïve, ungentrified woman from the poverty-pocked American South.

Yet it had been much more than a failed love affair. During their brief time together, Qasim had opened the gates that led her here when they parted. He'd led her to who she was meant to be. How grateful she was to him.

Where is Qasim now? Is he still in Lebanon? Damn that Jamal for taking him back into a hopeless situation, right back into the civil war as it renewed itself. He'd lied to her, probably to Qasim, too, so that he could convince Qasim to return to home and country. He'd done everything he could to break them up.

Ghosts of the past. Memories a decade old. It's up to her now. She's facing a different kind of war. She knew what she was getting into when she began the negotiations with Biel in Nairobi. She's still amazed he let her come here to Camp Piecewood. He's using her as a pawn, just like the children. She'd suspected as much in Kenya, but she'd come anyway, full of humanitarian zeal in her belly. She must remember that this is simply who Biel is.

Was there some clue she's missed that could get them out of this stalemate?

Chapter Two:
Displacement

March 16, 1991
Piecewood Displaced Persons Camp

After her morning run, Dianna prepares her hut for a visit from her colleagues from the delegation in Juba. She lines up schoolbooks in a corner, pulling them all to the front so everyone can view the titles on the bindings, and shoves her personal belongings in her trunk.

She wipes off the dust from the mosaic enameled box Qasim gave her, which she brought here, full of his old postcards, searching for guidance. She gets none. Just pictures of palm trees and scribbles from hotels in the Middle East: today, Riyadh, tomorrow, Amman. Never Beirut. He couldn't get into the airport because it was always being bombed. To the young Dianna, his notes seemed careless, even disingenuous, and the photos seemed all too ordinary for a place as foreign as the Middle East was to her then. She recalls wondering if the entire region was all pools and palms. How could she have imagined today's connection between the States and the Middle East? And how that connection really was always there.

"What's that?" A boy stands in her doorway.

"It's a box. It's sentimental. It was a gift."

"Sentimental?" The boy reaches for her box.

"Please don't touch it," she says.

"But it is beautiful. What is inside it?"

"Please don't touch it. It is from someone I love."

"Is he dead?"

"I—I don't think so."

"Oh." Sudanese citizens understand not knowing if a loved one is dead or alive.

"Please don't touch it. It's my most treasured possession."

"Not a cow?"

She smiles. "No, I do not own cows here."

"No school?"

"No, no school today."

The boy scampers out, thrilled to have some free time.

She puts the box down, feeling deflated. He hasn't listened to her. She'd warned all the boys there'd be no school today. Maybe he'd been daydreaming. Yet do they see school as persecution? It's obvious what she's teaching isn't sinking in.

She's excited to meet someone, anyone, who might help her help these children. Juba is not far from here, but it might as well be in another country. She's thrilled to have the delegates' support, nervous about their scrutiny. Her stomach growls from butterflies. It's already given up growling from hunger. She'll have her first work performance review today.

No humanitarian went into Southern Sudan with blinders on. Everybody knew their efforts could prove futile and that they faced some form of danger. They also knew that whatever they accomplished might be eradicated the next day. The World Bank had pulled funding for development due to Sudan being a "poorly performing country." Sudan, constantly at war with itself, had low incomes, weak policies, and a tattered infrastructure. Its leadership had neither the capacity nor inclination to strengthen any of it.

Dianna is lucky to be here. If she can show the U.N. some success with the boys here, she may get a head of delegation position in a safer place. She might have been their last approved funding in this country. She needs to impress them, show them she's competent, all while pressing upon them the urgency of what's unfolding around her, without seeming alarmed herself. She would. She must.

As only humanitarians could, they all held hope. Conflict is big business; funding peaks anew every year. So, this tiny group, including Dianna, had permission to be in the country to prepare a few of its young citizens socially and economically, two things Sudan had seen little of in years. She was part of a tiny, last-ditch effort. Meanwhile, warring factions have begun using food aid to attract civilians to their camps, their sides, and their way of seeing.

Despite years of development attempts, most development professionals wanted to look the other way simply because little has changed in this country. Neither the workers nor the Sudanese leaders wanted to own up to their mistakes. No one—leader or humanitarian—wanted to admit failure. No one, not even the villagers, knew how to solve the war and famine that led to more war and famine. More than a million killed and close to that many refugees. What's left in the South is soldiers, their boys who are soldiers in training, and civilians being held hostage for food. It's difficult to determine who is the enemy of whom. What started as a North/South civil war became a religious war and now is largely tribal. More than ten nongovernmental agencies are supposed to meet civilian needs. Yet often, they can't, or won't, or their efforts are thwarted by governments, militaries, or even civilians.

She calls her few colleagues over from the make-shift warehouse for a brief meeting, all local except the Ugandan woman called Aria. "We need to be very presentable today," she says. "Staffing is at an all-time low, partly because no one wants to be here or because they've been ordered out for their own safety. Plus, you experienced a major malaria outbreak right before I arrived." She doesn't mention that rumors of a new disease, worse than AIDS, are everywhere. The refugees, the citizens, the soldiers, and the NGO workers all subsist in a soup of fending for oneself. People are tired of begging for assistance that doesn't come. They are beyond depression. They are numb.

"We know, madame," Aria says.

"Thank you, Aria. Just a reminder. I know how hard you all work. We need more staff here."

One of the men sighs, a tired sigh that reminds her they've heard that before.

The aid agencies have congregated outside Khartoum, where most families have fled, where their efforts will make a small difference. Few children attend school here because they cannot concentrate with empty, distended bellies. That's why *she's* here to start the education process again, until the next battle. The duration of these refugee-camps-turned-settlements extends decades. It's difficult to differentiate between the displaced from their supposed caregivers. She and her colleagues must often remind themselves why they do what they do.

"I'll stop pestering you after a couple of visits," Dianna says. "It's my first delegation visit. I haven't seen them in a while. They're 70 kilometers away."

Aria shuffles her feet. She's ready to go back to work.

"We hope you enjoy their visit, madame," another staff worker says.

"Thank you, Mohammed. I will. And you can call me Dianna."

"Yes, Madame Dianna. Will they bring food?"

"Yes, Mohammed. They told me they would."

"Let us pray they do not get attacked."

When she met Ted and Mirembe at the headquarters, they'd told her a truck would deliver food monthly. Today was the day, but bandits rob food trucks all the time. Those who own the most food will win this war, while the others starve. They've got enough to get by for the short term. It's almost all U.N-supplied, so it's not tainted or rotting. This camp gets visited by workers from the neighboring camp once a week, and they bring a little food. Their own water is fresh from a recently built well. She's lucky they have water. She looks over at the well, wondering how deep they had to dig to hit liquid. They had more likelihood of finding oil than water. It barely exists here, instead only war and a constant search for food. This is as close to civilization as most can get.

"Doctors will come next week," says Sam, who usually deals with water and sanitation. He's been limping for three days.

"You've put antiseptic on your cut?" she asks. He nods that he has, like, 'why is some young white woman telling him how to care for a wound.' If he's thinking about doctors, he must suspect infection.

Doctors Without Borders come through every other month, a pastor or priest trailing behind the physician. Otherwise, qualified local doctors are as scarce as food.

The only woman here is Aria from Uganda. They are hitting it off. No Americans, but a man, Ted from the U.K., is at the delegation. Mirembe's Sudanese. In fact, all her other colleagues are Sudanese, displaced themselves, just trying to live on subsistence.

She gives them last-minute assignments and puts on a clean pair of jeans, at least as clean as possible without a washing machine. She skims her letters home one last time. They remind her of those three-sentence postcards Qasim used to send her from the Persian Gulf. They didn't say much. They couldn't. Everything interesting would be censored and redacted anyway.

She seals and addresses the envelopes, drawing a heart with *xo* on the outside.

●　　●　　●

The plane lands, kicking up dust and breaking rocks on a makeshift runway, with much fanfare from the inhabitants. It bears the emblem of the World Food Program. The children follow the plane, excited, chanting in tribal languages. They form an assembly line, and the men from the plane hand them each a bag and walk with them to the building that stores the food to ensure they don't steal any for their families or militia.

After they deliver bags of grain to the warehouse and check the well, Mirembe and Ted invite her and Aria and Sam, their two local hires, to the coolest hut, and they go over figures: How many fed, how many provided kits, how many readers in her classes. She fibs a little. Statistics allow the area to get more food and supplies delivered. She counts all the boys who show up each day, even if their reading is not improving. She's proud to have given out all the kits they provided, and all without conflict. The boys' arm circumference is increasing, too, meaning they are well nourished.

"Where are the women, Dianna?" Mirembe asks. "The mothers?"

"I'm not sure." Dianna shrugs. "It was like this a month ago when I arrived. The boys seem to like and respect me, as they would some benign family member. The young ones still value reading, even though it's next to impossible for them to concentrate on it. Most of them have forgotten any Arabic they learned. The youngest never learned any. That makes it easier for them to learn to read the English in your books, at least. I'm not sure why we're teaching them English?"

"English books are what we have access to, Di. We're trying to find some Arabic books for the next delegate." It's as though Ted's warning her of something, but she can't decipher what.

"Why are you asking about women?" she asks Mirembe. "You mean they've taken the women away?"

"We need to fly over the area to ascertain what's going on," Ted says before Mirembe can answer. Why didn't they do that on the way in? Maybe because they were hitchhikers on a plane filled with food. The different sections of the U.N. weren't always friendly with one another, and NGOs were all vying for status. Her organization was the lowest of the lot.

"And how are you doing, Dianna?" Mirembe asks. She leans toward Dianna as though she expects a confidence.

It's unwise to confide in just anyone here. She did that once five years ago in Tanzania, and she almost lost her job. She'd love a friend, but she keeps her distance. She's recently heard that Mirembe was in Biel's tribe before they both went to England for their education. Tribal blood runs thicker than any gender, any education, any job. Especially any other tribe, and they might think her "American" affiliation is the worst tribe yet.

"It's everything I expected and more," Dianna says, giving Mirembe a knowing wink. "It will take time, but I've seen progress."

"Your living conditions are safe?" Mirembe asks, her face full of fatigue. They both know "safe" is not a common word in Southern Sudan.

"So far, except for sidestepping the random poisonous vermin," Dianna says with a chuckle. "I have a method of waking up in the morning to ensure I don't get any bites."

"Yes, you've spent time in Africa." Mirembe nods. "I would assume you'd know all about insects, reptiles, and wild animals. I was speaking about the boys, or even worse." She lowers her voice to a whisper. "The men."

Is she truly concerned or pumping her for information? Maybe she can rely on her a little. "There is a young boy, too young for here," she says.

Again, that look of concern, a flutter of lashes from Mirembe. "Do you know his name?"

"Khalil. He knew a little English already."

"Let me look into it." Mirembe squeezes her hands together and looks down at her lap. She must know something. "Have you seen soldiers?"

She didn't know what to say to Mirembe when the men seemed to all be under eighteen. "Not with any certainty," Dianna says. "I don't know how they could give up any food here for the military. The 'men' here I don't know are really teens. Have you seen any training fields around here? I suspect there are some."

"If there are, we'll find them," Ted says. "I didn't see anything suspicious when we flew in, but we need another go-'round."

"Do you think any food is being kept from the people here?" Dianna asks, hugging her knees to her chest.

"We have proof that millions of U.S. dollars in food donations are being diverted somehow. We think the food may be being sent to a man named Riek Nassir, who is vying for Garang's position." Ted scratches his nose and bats away a fly.

"I think I might have heard that name," Dianna says. A shiver traverses down her back. "Only once, from an older boy."

"Boy?" Mirembe's forehead creases with concern.

"I guess the adults live elsewhere." Dianna doesn't believe her own words, but she doesn't want to get sent home. "The boys come and go at will. I do my best to corral them, but sometimes it doesn't work." She finally decides to tell them what's been worrying her. They are the only ones she's got to tell. "I suspect they're off doing combat training. Biel leaves me be most of the time. But I am concerned about that small boy I just met. I told you; his name is Khalil."

Mirembe's eyes flutter wide. She must know who Dianna is talking about. But again, Ted interrupts, launching into a long monologue about the fighters and their positions. He finally winds down his speech and looks straight at Dianna. "You're doing a fine job, Dianna, considering the circumstances. We may need to move you out. It looks as if the Sudan People's Liberation Army is splintering, and leader John Garang may be losing what little control he had. Have you seen any food being hoarded or shipped?"

"I don't know how they could give up any food from around here," Dianna says. "But the boy . . ."

"We cannot help a single individual," he says. "The situation is tenuous, and you must keep up appearances until we have a better idea of what's happening behind the scenes."

"The boy . . . Khalil . . . seems to be special to Biel. Biel may be abusing him. At the very least, he's making him into a child soldier."

"There are so many of them," Ted says. "We do what we can."

"As do I," Dianna says, staring him straight in the eye. "I wouldn't want a single individual to be on my conscience."

"Good," Ted says. "You do what you can, Di. Jolly good work. Keep it up, Di." He rolls the long paper of figures up like a map and stuffs it back in a cylinder. "Need any supplies?"

That's what Sudan is to Ted. Statistics. "Some shampoo would be nice," Dianna says. "And more writing paper." She hands Mirembe her tissue-thin airmail letters to send back home to her sister Mary Ann who's caring for their mother and Leah, her old friend from her New York days. She's reassured them that all is well, sending her snapshots of the children, the camp, and her dwelling. She wants to tell them about what's happening here, but she can't without other eyes reading it. Instead, she makes it sound like one big adventure. She's stuffed some dollar bills left over from her travels in Mary Ann's note, but they'll probably get stolen on their way to her.

"Will do," Ted says. "You know where to find us." He takes her work performance review in hand and taps her on the shoulder with it. "We'll be in touch as soon as we make a decision about your staying or leaving." She takes it from him with a thank you that she doesn't feel.

"I want to remain," Dianna says, emphasizing the last word. "I only just began working with these children."

Ted sighs. "Do you think you're the first to say that, Di? We must keep you safe." His eyes roll up to the hut's roof as though he's searching for the heavens. "Even if it's from yourself."

The pair turn away, walk out of the hut, and with that, they are gone, almost as rapidly as they showed up. She feels relieved to still have her job but near tears from the vacuous loneliness she always feels here. There is so much turnover in these situations that the people training her don't know much more than she does about a mission, but at least they are company. Ted might not even be here next month.

Mirembe knows something, though. She hopes she can get her alone. She can't let Biel realize she wants to talk to her. She'll have to figure out a way to get to the delegation.

She sits in the shade, watches them walk to the plane, climb on board. The propeller twists, gains speed, and the plane launches into the sky. She takes a drink of water, but it's as if her mouth is almost too parched to swallow. For the first time since she's gotten to this camp, she's afraid.

She rises from the makeshift table and wipes the dust off it and her once-clean jeans. Maybe someone else will return in a few weeks with better news. Till then, she has the Sudanese staffers to ask questions of. They're prone to silence, but perhaps they'll get friendlier when they realize she's not trying to throw a wrench in Southern Sudanese politics, which all revolves around finding enough food to eat.

CHAPTER THREE: STALEMATE

April 20, 1991
Piecewood Camp, Southern Sudan

The boy sleeps beside her. His firm muscles rise and fall, rise and fall, in the perfect bliss of sleep. The boy's nap may get them found out; even a quick rest is a risk that will not bode well for her or him. Their clandestine reading meetings could mean her expulsion from this camp and this country. Khalil could cost Dianna her job. Something in the boy's eyes propels her on. Something about his keen desire to absorb words, roll them around on his tongue, swallow them whole.

"Khalil?" she almost whispers, sad to disturb him but knowing he will soon be missed. "It's time to go back." She touches his child shoulder, so slender yet so strong, like a bird's wing.

Khalil stirs and opens his eyes, squinting first, then wider. "Dianna!" He beams and hugs her. He rises and skips out of their cinderblock palace into the harsh sunlight.

He now arrives at her dwelling every day before supper. His minute body hauls a burden on his shoulders—an urn, blackened pot, or less often, *duna*, the local grain. The grain is probably stolen from the villagers, although Biel would say it was a donation. The villagers who are missing it most likely suspect the Northern troops of pilfering. The Northerners are sometimes the culprits, but seldom do they leave the farmers or fishermen alive to tell the story. The Southern soldiers take it as their due but leave the villagers alive to tell the tale.

"Khalil! Come back! We haven't read yet!" she shouts. He trots back with a teasing grin.

Dianna sits crisscross-applesauce on the dirt floor next to her only window. Khalil wedges into her lap, all elbows, ribs, and knees. He knows the alphabet now and some small words with two to three letters. They are reading *The Cat in the Hat*, one of the few of her own children's books she was able to haul with her. This book is special because she read it to her younger siblings. The sun filters onto the faded aquamarine book, tattered and stained with juice on the page introducing Thing One and Thing Two.

Khalil smiles as she reads the clever rhymes, and her heart beats out its own poetic tattoo:

Khalil is not yet old. He is fresh and new.

Khalil is not yet seasoned. He is hopeful.

Khalil gets off her lap, pacing, listening, then bounces on her mattress. Her rusty cot, draped with a thin quilt her grandmother made in her youth, lines one entire wall. Books piled beside the bed make a nightstand, lanterns decorate every corner, and a small cook-stove, with a rickety chair in front of it, takes up the middle of the room. And it's enclosed. She doesn't need to sleep outside under a blanket of mosquitoes, remaining half vigilant of every wild call of the night.

"The sun did not shine. It was too wet . . ." Dianna begins. "Khalil, repeat the sentences after me." She points to the words with her fingers and repeats them.

"The sun was . . ." Khalil begins but falters. "Why did the sun not shine?"

"It was raining." "So, we sat in the house all that cold, cold wet day," she continues.

"Oh." Khalil seems satisfied with her answer. Sated from reading, he yawns. His head rests on her upper arm. "Does it rain in your village all the time?" He points at the picture of two steadfast children gazing out the window at the pelting rain. "Why they sad?"

Again, another term that is difficult to explain to someone who has never known it: boredom.

Khalil is not yet wounded. He is compassionate and kind.

Khalil is not yet full of contempt. He is filled with love.

"Are they sad at the rain? Do the rain make sad?" His gaze is at once penetrating and fervent.

"Khalil, do you know how you feel at the end of a long day of work?" she asks him.

"Yes," Khalil replies. "Very tired."

"Yes," she says. "These children feel tired of sitting like you feel tired of working."

"Oh." Khalil grins, and she continues.

"I sat there with Sally. We sat there, we two."

"I like sit with you," Khalil says.

Dianna hugs him. She is beginning the seventh page, pointing at every word, with Khalil trying to repeat each line when the sun is suddenly blocked. Khalil's body immediately stiffens, and she remembers a wood thrush caught in her childhood badminton net. It was the same stiff feeling next to her skin, followed by a shudder. His tension makes her shudder, too. It must be Biel. Khalil's fear pierces her, lodges in her chest. For a moment, she dares not look up. She fully expects a slap or for him to knock them both across the room. Just like her mother used to.

Khalil is not yet us.

He is alive, in body, in spirit.

She looks up, determined not to show any fear she feels echoing through the stillness.

"Yes?" She looks at Biel's face, but it is completely in shadow. *She must protect Khalil, protect his spirit.*

He stands there for a moment, then in the next, comes and knocks Khalil into the corner. The back of his fist comes up again, and he steps toward Dianna, and she utters a gasp. The hand comes down, but it stops in midair. He goes over to the corner and starts to shout in a language Dianna has never heard before. He throws Khalil against the doorframe, and Khalil dashes out, whimpering. Biel stands there, catching his breath. A fault line of sweat divides his right temple, his pulsing jaw. She can see his eyes now, and they beat with rage. His finger comes up to wipe his upper lip, and she can see blood on its tip. She wonders, with the detachment of a person who has just been in a terrible accident, whether it is Biel's blood or Khalil's.

He stands, and she continues sitting, staring at one another like two cornered cougars. She begins to count silently, not from anger, but as though she is counting sheep, trying to find the calm of a sleepy night. It is nowhere to be found.

"Miss Calloway," Biel hisses between the gaps in his front teeth. "You come highly recommended. I am sure this will not look good on your otherwise impeccable record, trying to subvert my boys against me. Your superiors will hear of this, as will mine."

She wonders who a warlord's superiors are but remains quiet and still.

"This is your last and final warning," Biel continues. "I am certain you understand me this time. Perhaps I was too vague in my previous request. Stay away from that boy. He is mine."

He just stands there, panting, his belly going in and out. Then he marches out of her dwelling. The sun catches the metal on his boots and shines into her eyes. Only when his marching boots have faded does she breathe again. She exhales and inhales three times. Then she falls to her knees and puts her head on her earthen floor.

● ●● ● ●

Dianna wakens during the wee hours. The moon has not yet tucked itself away beyond the horizon. She gets up and paces, wondering if Biel is up, too, trying to figure out what to do with her. She must act fast before he does.

The night birds are calling, moaning. Her belly is an empty pit. No, it is a place of fire and dark ice. A lagoon of remorse, with a ferocious rusty orange projectile of frozen lava jutting out, piercing the ice it once inhabited. She always thought she was the abandoned one, first by family, then by men. Yet she's abandoned Khalil in the worst possible way. She'd not listened to Biel. She'd kept reading to Khalil.

She's made the wrong moves from the beginning. This must be what a lioness felt like, or another great animal on the plain, watching a hyena take down her cub. If you had taken another route, trained your offspring better, weaned him sooner, then you and he would be the ones making this kill. Instead, your baby is gone, gone forever. She could have saved him five minutes ago, let him leave without reading with him. Now, it is too late.

None of her years of humanitarian work in Africa prepared her to negotiate with Biel, and yet, she must. Her five years as a menial researcher at the Metropolitan Museum of Art inched by in second-hand increments and did not prepare her for a displaced-persons camp in the middle of the rural Sudan South. All she'd done was type little green catalog cards that recorded objects of art and history for five long years. She'd discovered a lot about people and places simply by discovering the provenance of a small earthenware dish. She recorded that dish description on dozens of tiny cards on a Selectric typewriter without correction tape, which led to her knowing that very dish was created and used here in Africa about 3,000 years ago.

In the last ten years, she's responded to famine by educating hungry children. She has responded to migration, not by building new shelters, but with education. She taught children who'd lost their homes, their parents, their siblings, to read. And now she's teaching reading—in English—in the thick of a simmering civil war.

None of her past prepared her for Sudan. Museum objects were not the people who created them. This was war, not a feeding station. The Sudanese knew how to build and create monumental art long before her own country came to be. They are ingenious survivors. This knowledge alone makes her respect every single person she meets. Biel is no exception. Yet what can she do to command his respect?

She's heard Biel is shrewd, and for this, she will need more than any previous research about this country. Biel is dangerously real. To deal with him, she will need what she learned in childhood. She learned to sidestep her parents' manipulations, to negotiate from their attempts to control her entire life, to make her do their will alone. She'll need to intuit his next moves; to do that, she must figure out his true intentions rather than his military strategy.

Who can help her? Who can guide her? The straight line of Qasim's Roman nose and the rest of his profile floats into her mind, the scars on his face betraying the scars on his soul. He would know what to do. Yet a decade and continents separate them, as well as their bitter words. He'd been damaged, but she'd played her own part in the injury. How she loved him. How he hurt her. How they hurt each other.

The moon starts to set. "Nowhere in this world or any world is child abuse moral. You may think you've got them all fooled, Biel. You may think you can get rid of me. Think again." It's her vow, with the moon as her witness.

She'll need to be patient, do whatever he says, go wherever he directs, take the first opportunity to ask for help. She can escape Biel if she's careful. Khalil cannot.

CHAPTER FOUR:
COLLATERAL DAMAGE

April 30, 1991
Near Torit, Sudan

"Where are we?" she asks the driver, who has a long twig hanging out of the right corner of his mouth.

"Near Torit," he mumbles and spits out the other corner through the rolled-down RV window onto steamy dust. The man, who tells her his name is "Driver" when she inquires, resembles a Biblical figure. Long flowing faded green robe. A turban-like hat rolled around a shiny bald head. A white beard as magnificent and nearly as long as the robe. No front teeth to speak of. Sandals that expose crooked toes that are miraculously cleaner than any other part of his body. The RV swerves to miss something hunched in the middle of the road, a child or animal she cannot determine. She looks back but can only see the RV's kicked-up dust trail.

Biel probably sent her on a wild goose chase to this nameless place "near Torit" to get rid of her for the day. Their tense relationship has taken a few steps backward since the day he found her with Khalil. Until then, she'd been a simple pawn in his chess game. Now she's come to threaten his "kingdom" because she'd begun to love a child who was valuable to him. She can't risk him reporting her "misbehavior" to her superiors.

It's simple courtesy to go from camp to camp to meet your colleagues, and she's been dragging her feet because she wanted to protect Khalil. Who's she kidding? She wanted to *see* Khalil. He is the light in her day.

She's hoping to find someone at the place he's sending her who will listen to her and decide to help him. At least this gets her out of camp, away from Biel's glare, so she might be able to plan a rescue.

"How much farther?"

Driver rolls down his window again, spits. "A little way longer." He doesn't bother looking at her in the rearview.

His allegiance is with Biel, and why wouldn't it be? He has food, transportation, and perhaps a bribe for driving her around.

She breaks into her stash of chocolate cookies from her sister Mary Ann. Once these treats are gone, it'll be months before she receives another care package. She probably won't eat again on this misguided journey. The RV hits a pothole and almost brings her cookies back up. She hopes she'll find a woman at this new camp.

The chocolate makes her nostalgic, though this is the first time she has ever missed "home." She imagines Mary Ann patrolling the aisles of a brand-spanking-new Piggly Wiggly. An entire aisle of cookies, crackers, and yet another aisle of chips. Real American chips, crunchy, crisp. Not stale. She smiles but feels it fade just as quickly because she brings herself up, quick, fast. It's been years since she thought of consuming food like this, gorging, gorging, not thinking to stop because all she can do is shovel, shovel it in. Oh, she is so, so hungry. And lonely. What would happen if she had more than this box of cookies? She might never stop eating.

Just another dichotomy of life in the clay plains of the South of Sudan, hunger so sharp that bulimia seems mild by comparison. Other paradoxes? Women in fancy lace dresses and patent leather high heels, fanning themselves in broken-down shanties, men driven in chauffeured Mercedes that kick up dust on the distended bellies of children fleeing the latest clash. What next?

Food has always been the major concern of her day in Sudan when she finishes in the classroom. There are two schools of thought about food in Africa. One espouses eating and drinking everything in sight the moment you hit the tarmac and worrying about the repercussions later. It's the only way, they would say. You're going to get sick eventually; why not get it over with? The other school of thought takes the high road, never eating anything that can't be peeled, ground, or cooked, and ensuring that every bottle of water is tamper-free. Africans fill up water bottles with lake water and re-sell them for a healthy profit. Inventiveness forced by necessity. She's taken her chances from the beginning. Now she has Biel's wrath to contend with as well. She wouldn't be surprised if he gave her poisoned water.

He wants to be rid of her. And perhaps he wanted to be rid of her from the first day they met, during their first chess match, those first two days negotiating in Nairobi.

They'd been sitting in the same room as the day before, which, if anything, was darker than ever. Sunlight filtered through red grime on the windowpanes where it could. A fly, mosquito, or another more menacing African insect fluttered in the corner of the cracked windowsill with a hiss rather than a buzz.

She knew language was key to this negotiation. Biel must be wondering how far she would take these young men. Would they still want to take up arms once they could win wars of words? Would they still bear the discontent that bound them to him when they could unlock the secrets of books? She was like a match on dry tinder to him.

His arguments were plausible, but she knew his underlying agenda. He was fighting a war—a war he did not instigate, with children as his only trainees.

"Someone must fight this war," he was saying. "If these children are sitting in tents reciting poetry, what good will they be on the battlefield? Most of these boys will need wisdom not borne in the pages of books. They will never finish school or enter a library. If they do not win the next battle, they will be running for their lives."

What would Qasim say? Nearly ten years of separation, and he's become more of her invisible mentor, a Jedi who whispers in her ear, than a lover. Even in his absence, she can hear his voice, see him sitting across a café table, rubbing his hands together.

*"Education, **education** is the way to turn this world around."*

"But Qasim, think of all the people who are educated who were not before. They've become more militant, haven't they?"

"You can't turn a country around overnight. You do it with education."

"Don't you remember those boys burning all those books last year? Where was it? Iran?"

"Dianna, sweetie, we are talking about an entire generation that has never tasted, let alone fully experienced, freedom. You have been free all your life. What do you expect of them? It takes time."

Time was of the essence now. "What hope is there for your society, Dr. Biel, without knowledge, without communication? Where the only motivation for your people comes from the butt of a gun? Someday this war will end. By then, thousands of these boys will be dead, thousands more without limbs. Where will their livelihoods come from then? How will they feed their families?"

Biel had frowned at her for an instant, then his stare glazed over. He pushed away his papers and placed two long fingers on the table. "Our literacy rates rival Morocco, Mozambique, even Egypt—"

"How many literate Sudanese inhabit the South?" Dianna leaned in.

Biel didn't take her bait. "Where does literacy take an agrarian society? Limbs or no limbs, words do not grow food. What hope is there, Miss Calloway, for 'my people' if they all lie sickening from poverty, hunger, and disease? What future is there if their land is taken away from them? What prosperity is there while others exist who would murder them in their sleep because of their darker skin? For that matter, what good is my doctorate to me in a place like this?" His chair tipped and righted itself, tipped and righted itself, with his weight.

Dianna pushed back from the table, but she suppressed the urge to rise. It had done him *some* good. Educated in the U.K., here he sat, the returned hero, staunch and proud, professing that education played no role in his position. Would he be a tribal leader without the ability to make mental connections with other people and places? Would his negotiations be as well-rounded?

She had said the only part of her thoughts she believed would not inflame him: "You may soon be the warlord of your tribe, Dr. Biel."

He pushed back from the table, a swift, scraping motion of chair and table legs. The table rammed against her ribs. "My father, and his father before him, were my tribe's leaders, Miss Calloway. Do not even attempt that argument."

Dianna reassessed the situation. "My sincere apologies, Dr. Biel. I meant no disrespect." A ticking in her throat told her it was time to close this deal, or it would be forever lost.

Rallying her last force of will and inspiration, Qasim's words flew from her as though she memorized them even as she disagreed with him. "Dr. Biel, education is the lifeline that will save your country. Once this war is over, and mark my words, it will be over; even in our lifetime, your people will need to build a society. They will need to get jobs, sign contracts, and pay bills. You cannot keep a nation undeveloped forever. This world is too small."

The Sudanese unclasped his hands yet again and put his fingers together in a pyramid. He pursed his lips and stared her down. She didn't budge. Suddenly, he clapped his hands together, fast, loud. The sound reverberated in the otherwise silent room. "I will need to think this over." He rose, almost knocking over his rickety chair, and turned on his heels, taking long strides to the door. He knocked, and someone turned a key on the other side that had locked them in or others out. It slammed shut behind him like a book.

When her contract arrived, it seemed he'd capitulated. Yet, even though he'd allowed her to join his camp, it was as if he'd figured out how to use her. She suspected Biel could read her philanthropic mind all along. But neither of them had put Khalil into their symbolic game of chess.

Time is in as short supply here as nutrition—time she does not have to help Khalil. Qasim always seemed to have time; he never negotiated unless he showed utter confidence. After close to a decade of field work with Operation Ready to Read, she can see that the books she shares will solve some ills and create others.

It was easier in Nairobi, where people wanted to read, and most spoke English, where some dishes were grilled. In contrast, Sudanese liked dipping and finger eating, spoke little English, and had no use for books.

● ● ● ● ●

Now, as the RV jolts to a halt, it seems she will be experiencing still further culinary adventure. She first notices two dead animals hanging from a tree by their legs.

They are small, like prairie dogs, though she knows prairie dogs don't live in Sudan. A flurry of women and children belch out of the open doors of three tiny huts, barely large enough to house one person. The people flow like a desperate river, undulating toward the car. Some stretch both arms out toward them, but most point to their mouths, making sure she knows they are hungry.

One small dark hand, half-cupped, taps at the passenger window.

It stays there for one or two heartbeats before it slides down the glass. Then it is gone. Dianna moves to roll down her window, to search him out, and Driver motions for her to stop. She obeys him and immediately feels remorse. The crowd rocks the RV, back and forth, almost as though their mad dancing will produce food or money or some higher assistance than earthly beings are capable of.

How many of them are there? Fourteen? As many as twenty? Thirty? She loses focus because when she opens the RV door and steps into this world that smells of dried plants and acrid sweat, the residents crowd around her, gesticulating, questioning her presence. Then one woman, a mother to four or five young girls and one baby boy, catches her eye. The boy will probably not make it to his next birthday. He leans his head with weak disinterest on his mother's chest.

An aid worker motions her toward him. He wears a baggy T-shirt with a ripped sleeve and indecipherable lettering from what Dianna supposes is another in a hodgepodge of nongovernmental organizations that she cannot decipher. His red beard is clipped, but his face, pink from heat, pours with sweat.

"I wouldn't go in that dwelling if I were you," he says as he pulls a cigarette out of his back pants pocket. "Got a light?"

Dianna shakes her head no. "Why shouldn't I go in there?" she asks as the woman drags her with surprising strength toward the hut.

"Some God-awful diseases in there, and you don't look like you're thin enough to be immune yet." He smiles, but his smile is not friendly.

"You've been in there, then?" Dianna disengages her arm from the distraught woman's grasp, folds her arms across her waist, and centers her eyes on his.

"Sure," he says, "but look at me. Get out while you still can."

She stiffens her back. She's had enough of men telling her where to go and what to do. That was what was wrong with humanitarian assistance. It was tied to a man's world. The word should have been "manitarian" instead of "humanitarian." She smiles, imagining a giant praying mantis feeding these people. Wasn't there something about the female praying mantis eating the man, or was that the female spider?

"Glad somebody still has a sense of humor." The man draws nearer, and she can smell his unwashed body. "Where are you coming from?"

"Somewhere just as bad as this," she says. "Just in different ways."

"Have to worry about your supplies being taken, just like the rest of us, I guess," he says, putting his hands behind his head and looking up at the heavens. "Just got some grain, but it'll be gone in a blink. What they don't shite out." He points toward a food container.

"Sure." She does not want this man to know where she is stationed. "Where is the head of your delegation?"

"Over there." The man motions to a tent not much bigger than her brother's old pup tent.

Dianna walks in that direction, and the woman—she's unable to determine her tribe—follows in tow.

"He's not going to tell you anything different than I did," the young man says with a bitter inflection. "Besides, it's your funeral," he shouts over his shoulder as he hauls a huge metal canister onto his shoulder and heads in the opposite direction through the sea of humans. They begin running toward the place where these foodstuffs will be distributed.

Everything, then, reduced to this container.

The older man greets her with a coffee-stained smile. His happiness to see her seems genuine. "Velcum," he shouts. "I am Tor. What brings you to this part of hell?"

Dianna recognizes the name and accent as Swedish, though the man looks and acts more Russian, big, and blustery.

Dianna walks in, and the woman follows, tugging at her shirt seam. Tor takes no notice of the African woman at all. "Sit," he says and motions to a small metal stool in the far corner of the tent. After her eyes adjust to the dim, filtered light, Dianna extends her hand, trying to look official.

"Thanks for having me," she says. "This is my first official mission away from my base. It's been months." She does not mention that she suspects Biel had an ulterior motive for sending her here. She sizes up Tor and decides to risk telling him about Khalil. It may be her only opportunity. She folds her hands in her lap. "I am in a sensitive situation," she says, then decides she is tired almost unto death of being diplomatic. "Surely you realize how many children are involved in this war."

Tor nods, one movement down only. "God, Lady, you're not one of these people who thinks you can save the children, are you? Look, these kids have a muscle-upper arm circumference that in any other country would mean they weren't worth even trying to save. And these are the lucky ones."

"At least they will die free. They are not slaves." Dianna works her watch round and round her wrist.

"What difference does it make if they are dead?" Tor sneers. "You don't know the first thing about why these people sell their children. Pawning has existed long before this war began and before you and I were born. We won't stop it. This continent is like Humpty Dumpty; a few containers of grain won't paste it together again. Besides, the great people in the United States want to send their old clothes instead of money for food. See that boy over there?"

He points through the open door to a passive three-year-old who sits in the dirt without anything on his bottom, a heavy wool cardigan draped around his shoulders.

"That's what they send." He hits his thighs with his hands, like a boy playing a bad game of slapjack, and rises. He limps across to her, his head bent against the tent's ceiling, and his limp suggests he has an artificial left leg. "Go back home, Lady. You won't find your dreams here. You won't be able to save them from themselves."

She frowns, watching him pace. He looks like an aging gazelle or kudu. He belongs here in a way the other man she met at the camp's entrance did not. Her heart lets off a few shavings of ice, and her voice is softer when she responds. "I don't want to save them all," she says. "I only want to save one."

"Argh!" Tor tears at his hair. "Don't think I haven't heard this one. It won't work. I know which camp you're in. We all know about you, Lady. Biel won't let you take one of those boys away for all the food containers you can beg off UNICEF or UNHCR. You must be U.N., right, with that kind of holier-than-thou attitude?" He twirls the tips of his curly hair, round and round, and she keeps rhythm with her watch band, round and round. She does not correct him.

She sits there, willing him to change his mind.

He does not.

"Look, the media will be here this afternoon. I must get ready for them. I've got to get the people who can still walk out to the feeding center, and I've got to get the dead bodies buried. The media has to get what it comes for; otherwise, you can forget about any more food. Not too much gore, just enough to pull at the heart strings. You can either help me, or you can leave. It is as simple as that."

"So, you will not help me get this boy an exit visa?" She looks into his red-rimmed eyes, and he licks his dry lips in answer. "His case is worse than most."

"What's 'worse' in this place?" He throws his hands up over his head.

The woman hurries up to her as if on cue, and Dianna wonders if she understands English after all. Perhaps she is a mole to discover what Dianna is made of or pump her for information. The woman pulls her towards another hut, a makeshift hospital. A cooking fire smolders in the room's center, and two elderly people, one male, the other female, huddle in one corner. They cough with malaria, or TB, or perhaps, worse, AIDS-induced pneumonia.

The prone elders in the hut's far corner must be the woman's parents. The woman's panicked look is so intense, it seeps into her every pore.

"Help?" the woman asks in English, her voice catching in her throat. Dianna can tell how this woman must have uttered this word many times.

"I am not a doctor," she apologizes, but she knows the woman will not understand her.

So, she walks to the old grandmother and places a hand on her heart. The woman could be as old as sixty or as young as forty-five, considering the toll famine has taken on her body. The ravaged look in her eyes indicates malnourishment has taken her mind and physical form. Her pulse is faint but rhythmic. Dianna closes her eyes and prays. Then she goes to the RV, gets her bottle of water, and places it against the ill woman's lips, then the man's. The woman sips and chokes.

The man does not respond. He probably only has a few more hours to live.

When she gets up, Dianna's eyes are moist, and she notices the moisture in the otherwise dry, dry creases of the daughter's eyes. "I have done all I can," she whispers, and the woman seems to understand beyond the words and breaks into wailing.

The other women come in and practically carry her out this door and through the door of the hut next door. They shove her to the floor and scurry around her, all the while chanting.

One woman walks up to her, inquiring, "Please?" She holds what might be a ladle. It contains some sort of animal body part she does not recognize. Probably sacrificed their last goat before it keeled over from heat exhaustion or got stolen in tomorrow's raid. She knows she has no alternative other than to gulp it down.

Humanitarians don't turn down gifts of food from villagers.

The taste is at once rancid and spiced. She does not chew, and it catches in her esophagus before plummeting down to her belly. This would have done some starving soul much more good. Dianna can feel the "meal" churning around already. She has never had this much of a visceral reaction, and she regrets she has given her water away. She bows to each woman, expressing her sorrow that she could not help further, and as soon as is conceivable, bolts to the RV. Driver is standing with the same stick in his lips. He barely widens his eyes when he sees her rushing toward the vehicle.

She kneels outside the passenger door and loses everything—the cookies, the animal organ, still almost whole, and this morning's breakfast, some sort of strange gruel with no name.

Tears stream down her face, not from emotion but in reaction to her body's attempts to void.

Strange how in times of physical crisis, our mind turns to those we love, even if we have blocked them, she thinks. Her mind drifts, to Qasim, standing, laughing, outside the pizza joint underneath the Chrysler Building's light blue neon glow. She remembers his hand on hers that night, and she wishes she could reach for it. How repulsed he might be by her condition, though. She is bone thin, or as thin as she gets, and if she has any intuition about what she has just imbibed, she is about to get thinner. Her clothes stick to her frame like a soiled bed sheet hanging on a clothesline in a bad storm. Her sunscreen stings her eyes, blurring her vision.

She crawls to the bumper of the RV and attempts to pull herself up. When she cannot, she puts her head in her hands and rocks back and forth. She used to think refugees she saw rocking were praying, but now she knows different. It is the comforting rock of the womb they were after, and now, so is she. Her hair is soaked, and the front of her blouse is stained. She tries to get up but retches again instead. She crawls to the driver's side out of sight. When she's done, Driver pats her shoulder, picks her up, and hauls her into the RV.

The next time she looks around, they are back in the middle of nowhere. Dust covers her face, her wet hair, her tongue. She gags again, and Driver slows.

"No need to stop. Not any more right now. I'm just gagging," she tells him.

"Maybe should have said 'no,'" he chides in his inaudible mumble.

"I could have?" she inquires, more rhetorically than for a real answer.

"Bad for you," he explains. "Sit in sun for days."

Dianna groans. She knows what she is in for. She must get back to Khalil before the disease takes hold. She's played out her chess game. She was the only person who could have saved Khalil. Now he has no one at all. And neither does she.

CHAPTER FIVE:
BETWEEN BORDERS

May 2, 1991
Nairobi, Kenya

"Khalil?"

Nothing.

"Khalil!"

Silence.

"Khalil!!"

Nothing but a strange humming.

Dianna wakes in a puddle of sweat, or is it blood? She's ripped starched sheets off a rough, hard mattress attached to a metal bed. The humming comes from a table fan.

Why is she in a bed?

She must get back to Khalil. Before Biel harms him. Has Biel trapped her here?

She tries to sit up but realizes she's restrained.

"I demand to be freed!" Her shout reverberates throughout the room, bouncing from wall to wall, back to her bed.

Is this prison? A holding pen? Are they going to deport her? Has she been arrested?

She flails around until she exhausts herself.

Her head is an anvil, and she can feel the blood pounding against the inside of her skull. Somewhere, her rational brain tells her she is very ill, yet this voice of reason is fading fast. A monster lurks just behind it, ready to take her down as soon as she is weak enough.

She heaves, but nothing is left to come up. How many days has it been, or has it only been hours? She longs for the cool tile of a Western bathroom, the smooth ceramic of an American Standard to cling to. She used to despise bathrooms. They made her recall a time when she was obsessed with food. How much she put in her body. How much she kept out. Or how much she rid herself of.

"Water!" Her shout comes out as a croak, and she tries to fill her lungs with air.

How basic her needs have become. She used to wish for a new car, a sapphire ring, or a double dip cone from Dairy Queen. Or Qasim. All of that is a luxury here, a memory, another life. With no water, how will she survive? Although any water that goes in one orifice will come out another—vomit from her gullet, cold sweat streaming from every pore. She blinks her eyes, hoping to wet them. The thought of dying of thirst is more than she can take.

She cries out again. And again, until she can no longer. She feels herself letting go, slipping into blissful darkness. A place where nothing matters, not even Khalil.

Sometime later, she cannot tell if it is night or day, arms lift her like an anesthetized animal and place her on what must be a stretcher. Her legs and wrists sway over its sides with each movement. "Careful!" she hears through what sounds like a drumbeat.

"Khalil!" she shouts. "Where's Khalil? We must find him!"

Her body sways back and forth with what little weight it still carries. Until it is still, and everything goes black.

When Dianna opens her eyes, she smells strong disinfectant. She notices that her stomach remains calm, cooperative despite the foul odor. She must be better. A breeze blows, touching the sides of gauzy mosquito netting. She could only be back in the relative safety of a Nairobi afternoon. In Nairobi, one minute, it is afternoon, and then just as suddenly, night falls, 6:00 p.m. each and every day. Afternoon. Night. No dusk. But it is not night for a while yet.

Nairobi's hushed blues and greens have replaced the harsh golds and oranges of the south of Sudan, and she sees Nairobi's red dust suspended in the air. Her sweat has made an outline on otherwise stiff white linens, starched so often they feel more like cardboard than cloth. She tries to move but cannot. Rags bind her wrists and ankles to the lime green rails of a decrepit hospital bed. She wants a shower and one of those ceramic toilets she dreamed of in her delirium. She doesn't know which she wants first.

"Hello?" Her call is a croak so meek she's not sure she heard it herself. Her next call echoes off antiseptic walls and the rin-tin-tin of a large bedpan, the only thing she can see through the netting.

The rags are loose enough for her to work her way out of. Once free, she strips the gauze and adhesive tape off her arm with no problem and is coaxing the needle out when she hears voices and reapplies the rags and tape. Yet the feet and voices shuffle past her room. The sound of a BBC radio station tries to make its way through mounds of static. "Years from now, men will speak of American and British heroism in the Gulf, as they do today of our cooperation in two World Wars and of peacetime and alliance," a male voice drones. Probably the voice of a U.S. Congressman, but the static makes it difficult to determine.

Papers shuffle through the static; still, no people show in her doorway, then another monotone voice begins. Why do newscasters always sound bored, even here in Africa? She is drifting off to sleep again when she hears, "Khartoum canceled U.N. flights and food convoys to Southern Sudan when it became suspicious that the U.N.-sponsored Operation Lifeline Sudan (OLS) relief program was benefiting the rebel Sudan People's Liberation Army (SPLA). There are signs that this program is getting back on track."

This announcement jolts her awake once more. She must get back to camp. This turn of events doesn't bode well for her program. "Hello?" she cries again, this time a fraction louder, but is still met with silence. Where is everyone? Surely, she's not in a private room in an African hospital. She shudders as reality takes her to a place she does not want to be. What if they gave her a transfusion?! Her insides reel, and she struggles to retain the calm that has recently been all she could feel. A catheter line extends up to her bladder and makes her notice she is wearing a makeshift diaper. She'll never be able to get up by herself.

At the seventh hello, a tall, thin man strolls into the room. A stethoscope twirls around his neck like a snake. His eyes meet hers, and he walks forward with a lighter step. "Mlle Calloway?" he inquires, as though they are meeting for coffee or an interview. He extends his hand, then laughs as he notices her inability to respond. He unties the rags, and she shakes her wrists, trying to get some feeling to return to them. He is well over six feet, and she cranes her neck, trying to look him in the eye.

"Where am I?" she requests.

"You have been quite ill," he says in lilting English. She thinks he must be Indian. His skin is not quite olive, not quite red, not quite bronze. His hair is dark and long and straight. He has a light mustache and a bit of grizzle at the tip of his chin. His eyes are dark and wide and layered with lashes. "You are in Nairobi, at the MSF field quarters clinic."

So that explained why she was alone. She's relieved and thankful for only a moment until Khalil, then Biel enters her mind again.

"What is wrong with me? Did I need a transfusion?" she asks and wants to ask more. She tries to focus on his face, which seems far away.

"You had cerebral malaria." His voice is almost a whisper. A soothing tone like a melody. He points his finger at her, not quite an accusing finger, more like he knows the answer to his next question. "Were you taking your prophylaxis?"

She gives him a grin with one side of her mouth, admitting her guilt. "Probably not as much as I should have been."

"It could have been that the pills combat one breed of mosquito and not another. Yet, it could also be you were not properly protecting yourself. These things do not work if they are taken intermittently. You were in the South of Sudan, yes?" He picks her wrist up to take her pulse, and reassured, picks up an ancient thermometer with a huge bulb, shakes down the mercury, and pops it into her mouth. She almost gags at the taste of the antiseptic, and he takes it out again. "*Ça va?*" he inquires.

Why is he speaking in French? He must think she is French.

She interrupts in English before he can jump to more conclusions. "I received Sudanese permission to conduct an Operation Ready to Read assignment at Biel's camp. I thought it would save at least a few of those boys. Yet, obviously, all I have accomplished is almost killing myself." He doesn't react to the hysteria in her laughter.

"How are you feeling?" he asks a second time.

"Just still a bit queasy, thanks." Her cheeks burn a bright pink, and for the first time, she is conscious of the disheveled, stinky mess she must present. Oh well, he must be used to patients in her state, perhaps much worse. So, she blurts out before she can think not to, "I presume I have you to thank for saving my life? Are you French?"

He laughs this time. He must laugh quite a bit. His laugh is melodic and tinged with a sarcastic, sharp pain. "I am French." He chuckles. "Have I lost that much of my accent? And yes, I am one of a league of hundreds you can thank for your improvement. You could have died before we had your *fievre* under control. It was 105 . . . that's correct in Fahrenheit, yes . . . when they brought you in." He pats her hand. "But we took care of you."

"But . . ." her voice trails off. It is not polite to mention his nationality, but he looks Indian. She thought he was an Indian from Kenya. How did she get to Kenya? "Who brought me in?" she asks instead.

With this, he looks away, out the window. "Some . . . gentle . . . men . . . some of Biel's bodyguards." He clears his throat. "Who . . ."

A pretty, cobalt-skinned nurse wheels a gurney into the room. An obviously pregnant woman with clipped red hair leans on her elbows, looking around. This is not to be a private room after all. "Hello," she says in a husky voice. "I am Anida. They should be letting me go soon. In fact, I shouldn't even be here. I have too much work to do." She laughs and coughs until her breath comes out in tiny puffs.

"Madame, please stay calm," the doctor says as he leaves the room. "Your baby needs air." He waves over his shoulder. "I'll be back to check on you after my appointments." His white scrubs trail behind him like a cloak.

The doctor had left, and she'd wanted him to stay. He made her feel safe and vulnerable all at the same time. She hasn't felt that way in a long time. She blushes. He's not there to see it, but the pregnant woman must have seen her expression. She's staring at Dianna.

"I am Dianna," she says and starts to extend her hand, but Anida interrupts her almost immediately.

"I have this parasite, and now I have some sort of bronchitis or pneumonia. All that, and my malaria could pop up at any time. These people won't be able to help me. I'll either live or die, like the rest of the people on this Godforsaken continent." Her pale blue eyes flash. "Shit!" She shifts in bed, and Dianna wonders if she should get up and find a nurse now that she's no longer restrained. This is the first time she has ever been a patient in a hospital.

"Are you alright?" she asks.

"Fine, just fine, considering what I've got to do before the end of the week," Anida proffers between coughs. "The baby is kicking up a storm. I'd probably be well if I could get some sleep. They can't rid me of this parasite until I deliver. They've given me every drug that's safe for the baby, and apparently, they're all completely safe for the parasite, too. Can't keep anything down. I'm gaining weight, though. Can't fit into any clothes, not even this hospital gown. They and my crazy husband have this insane idea of keeping me here until I deliver. That's at least another two months! As soon as my blood pressure goes back down, I am out of here!" She sputters, catches some air, and starts another coughing jag.

"I know how you feel," Dianna mutters.

Anida's choking diminishes. "What are you in for?"

This strikes Dianna as immensely funny, and she begins to chuckle, then belly laughs until she is close to tears again. Even though it hurts. Anida giggles along with her, stopping each time she triggers a cough. Maybe this *is* a prison; after all, her arms were just bound. Finally, she gasps, "Malaria."

"Get used to it if you're living here," Anida quips, and they laugh again.

"Cerebral malaria."

"Oh, you're lucky to be alive then."

"Where's your husband?" Dianna asks as the nurse brings her some applesauce and attaches some sort of electrical device to Anida's legs, which she assumes stimulates circulation.

"Oh, my husband is Egyptian," Anida says by way of explanation. "He wouldn't be bedside with me."

Dianna gobbles the first two bites of food, then thinks better of it. She is starving, but the taste of food is almost unfamiliar. She vows that if she makes it through this, she will never make herself vomit again.

What was she thinking of so long ago? The world is upside down here, with people unable to gain weight as much as they try and people on her side of the world unable to lose weight despite millions of dollars and oceans of tears. It is strange that when people are dying of thirst and starvation, their bellies get bigger and bigger. And while she was trying to rid herself of, what—food, weight, past burdens—her stomach remained flat, no matter how much she ate, no matter how much she purged.

She couldn't starve herself to death in America if she tried. Here, though, all it took was a few nights without one little malaria pill. Dianna runs her hand over her abdomen. Is it her imagination, or is it a bit swollen? She's in no condition to leave. The doctor is right.

But Khalil. She's already lost so much time! To whom can she turn for help? She's not even in Sudan! She does not like the face that floats into her mind. It is Qasim, with his tanned olive skin, tapered hands, and the scars on his face and soul. How she loved him. How he hurt her.

As she spoons the applesauce into her mouth and sips mango juice, Anida tells her story. She is Danish; she met her husband while they were both in school, and they came to Africa to farm. Anida has one child already, a little girl, who is helping out the gardener and her *aya* right now. Her husband is an agricultural engineer, and they are some of the first in the region to harness solar energy for power to irrigate their crops. "So, you can see, I need to be there, and this is crimping my style. Two more months and things will be back to normal in Malarial Equatorial," she sniggers, then winces and rubs her stomach. "I hope this one is a boy so I can stop," she says and begins to cough again.

Dianna leans back, fatigued from the effort of eating and listening. Anida continues to jabber away, but Dianna is in another world now. Her mind, body, and spirit are working on processing the applesauce, so smooth, rich, and life-giving. She knows she will be all right. She dismisses asking Qasim for help. Who knows where he is. She can do this without him as soon as she has an ounce of strength in her body. Because she's not alone. She carries Qasim's lessons within her.

Her senses are returning to her, yet she can barely stand, let alone travel. She can't get out today or tomorrow, but the minute she's able, she's going to the American Embassy and demanding their help to rescue Khalil.

CHAPTER SIX:
NEGOTIATIONS, STALLED

May 31, 1991
American Embassy
Nairobi, Kenya

The American embassy is a big building, near the American Express Building, a landmark in this part of the world for every nationality. Still, Dianna walks right past. It is on a street full of large multi-level buildings, the corner of Selassie and Moi Avenues, and anything on an avenue dubbed "Moi" is bound to be big in one way or another. Dianna has seen the Kenyan leader's picture in every official building and many homes in Kenya. The people say it is not obligatory, that they hang it from pride and respect. Still, the only place Dianna remembers its absence is Karen Blixen's home, a vestige of colonial history, a memorial to her book *Out of Africa*, not of modern Kenya.

The women behind the counter wear navy blazers and bright batik sarongs, and they giggle with each other as she approaches, twittering about today's upcoming dinner. "Excuse me." Dianna places her hands on top of the counter.

"May I help you, Madame?" A young girl—when did she begin thinking of women in their early twenties as young girls—leans over the high counter and looks down on Dianna.

"I am an American seeking to obtain a visa and ultimately a green card for a young Sudanese boy, a minor. I can prove that his life is at stake." Dianna fishes in her satchel for her professional identification and passport and sets them on the counter, which is level with her shoulders.

The girls whisper behind the counter and give each other looks that must have some meaning for them, if not for Dianna. "Madame, this is Kenya, not Sudan." An ingratiating smile tugs at the sides of the taller woman's lips.

Dianna leans forward over the counter to determine what they are doing with her documents. "Of course, this is Kenya. Do you think there is any remote possibility of my getting this young boy an exit visa in Khartoum?" Her voice breaks. She is still weak from her time at the hospital.

The women, like birds, get up, sit down, look through a directory, and get up again. "Let me see, Madame," remarks the younger one. "I'll see if I can find someone to speak with you." They obviously have no desire to pursue the matter any further. She has become a bother, and she is an American bother, the worst sort. "May I have your passport?" the older woman asks. She glances at the photo, back at Dianna, picks up a sheet of paper, stamps it, and takes both with her to another side room.

Dianna strolls to the windows and sits on a leather window seat. She counts the stars on the huge American flag hanging on the wall above her. She is on her third round of "fifty" when the woman returns. A well-dressed American man with a crew cut follows her. "Miss . . ." He looks down at her passport. "Calloway? I understand you have identified a refugee in need of American assistance?"

"Not exactly a refugee." Dianna offers her hand, hoping beyond hope that this man can help. "I'm not even certain he is a displaced person or even an orphan, but his life is in danger."

"What is his name?" the man asks without introducing himself.

"And you are?" asks Dianna, raising her eyebrow in a practiced manner. He needs to understand she knows the steps in this bureaucratic dance.

"I'm Edwin Davis. You're in Kenya on business?" He raises his brow to match hers.

She likes this man, but she remains on guard. "Yes."

"You're with?" He holds his hands together like they are glued.

"I am with Operation Ready to R-E-A-D." She inflects each and every letter. When he interrupts, she is ready to explain how her organization fits into the U.N. and nongovernmental agencies.

"Good God, there's no way I can keep up with all the NGOs," he says, and his hands fly into the air.

"We've been around a long time." She's not budging.

He waves off the explanation. "All you international organizations are the same, regardless of the acronym. And you're teaching this young man to read?" He sighs, but she is uncertain whether from impatience, exasperation, or sheer fatigue.

"I'm trying to, but his commander tells me I'm not to be near him."

The embassy man's voice gets low and deep. "His commander?"

"I am teaching at what I believe to be a military training camp," she says. "It educates them, just in case they find a way out." She laughs in desperation and grief, surprised but pleased that he laughs with her.

"Miss Calloway, I appreciate the delicacy of this situation, but what do you want from me? I am in a completely different country, a completely different region of Africa." He wrings his hands and steps away from her. "If I were you, I'd call your Ready people and get on the next plane home. Do they know the situation on the ground?"

Dianna holds up her hand to stop him and give further explanation, but he takes another step back.

"There is nothing I can possibly do with relations as strained as they are," he says. "I am truly sorry. I wish you luck." With that, he returns her passport, turns around, and practically bolts back into the small vestibule that must lead to offices.

Dianna was not expecting a warm reception, but still, disappointment seeps down through her bones. She wants to sink down onto the floor but is still too much a professional to do so. He's right. Khalil isn't her son. Khalil may be dead already, or worse. She's been gone almost a month. There's little she can do, but if there's a way, she'll find it. She walks up to the counter and hands the older of the two women an underused calling card. "Please call me if anything changes," she requests, and the tall woman gives her a sympathetic look.

The man comes out of the vestibule. "I did some checking. There is not a thing we can do unless you get him out of the country. That doesn't seem likely now, does it?"'" He seems to be considering if her goal is truly impossible, then groans. "Give me a day to make some more calls."

Dianna nods her head yes. She wants to jump for joy. "I'll make another appointment. Thank you." She wants to pursue this, but she is dizzy. She wishes she were hungry, but she doubts she can eat more than half a piece of fruit.

She turns to go. Then stops.

Her peripheral vision has locked on to something, at once foreign and familiar, the tweed of a jacket. Her chest feels as though it is about to implode. Amazing how she can recognize this man by the sleeve of a jacket after all this time. A decade.

Qasim is walking and talking to someone, raising his hand for emphasis. She can't see who it is at first, but eventually, a young American man, a military cut having stolen most of his red hair, comes into view. The man is trying to keep pace with Qasim, even though his legs are longer. A young woman keeps pace on Qasim's other side, holding a stack of notebooks. Her eyes connect with Qasim's, and she tilts her head to one side and laughs. A scythe cuts through Dianna's heart.

Good grief! What does she expect? That he has remained celibate all these years? Just because she has locked herself away from men in that way and been married to her work? Just because he was once married to his? She reminds herself that people change, and it has been a decade. Perhaps he won't even notice her.

Qasim is almost out the door when he looks up, startled, like an animal meeting the dust kicked up by her speeding Land Rover in the bush. He steps toward her. Stops. Starts again. With each step, the dust lifts, and his eyes, darker than any gazelle's, lock with hers. Dianna looks down at her chewed fingernails and smooths her long skirt, which hangs down to her ankles. She wears it out of modesty, but she can tell from Qasim's gaze that he is taking her gesture in quite another way. He stands in front of her for a long time, staring. She thinks perhaps she has caught him off-guard for the first time in her life. She would be pleased to have the upper hand if she weren't in such shock.

The sun finds its way into the big open room and dances off the flags and the tile floor. No one moves until the man asks Qasim if he knows her. Qasim answers yes, as he lifts a finger at her, then waves on his two companions to go ahead without him.

"Shame on you," he says soft and low. "Shame on you for not letting me know where you were." When Qasim pulls Dianna toward him, Dianna kisses Qasim on both cheeks before he can kiss her. After he exchanges this greeting, his gaze rests on her face. "Dianna," he says, simply, sadly.

"Qasim." She laughs with nerves in every vocal cord and pats his shoulder. "What brings you here?"

He stands there, looking at her. "You have lost weight," he says.

She laughs up the scale and back again. She hopes it does not reflect her parched throat or her shaking hands. "Sudan will do that to a person," she answers.

"Sudan?" Qasim practically shouts the word. "You shouldn't be in Sudan! It is unsafe!"

Again, she laughs to hide her discomfort—and because she can tell it affects him. Then, mirroring his low tone, she says, "No one tells me what to do these days."

He takes a step back and adjusts the sleeve of his jacket, which brings memories flooding back. One by one, her vertebrae stiffen as each memory hits her.

She changes the subject. "What are you up to?"

"I'm still with the U.N. My father died recently. I asked for a while off."

"I'm sorry. Why are you in Nairobi?" He's confusing her and making her feel sad for him.

"I've just returned to work, and they've assigned me sub-Saharan Africa. I'm getting debriefed." He tugs at his sleeve again, and her eyes light on a shiny cufflink. Her knees almost buckle. She recognizes that cufflink.

"I'm sorry," she says, and when he looks a bit confused, she adds, "About your father. I know how close you were."

His eyes well up, that old familiar sensitivity coming out of a usually impenetrable machismo.

"Are you all right, Dianna?" he asks and catches her arm.

"Fine, fine, yes," she says. "I've only just been released from hospital."

"My, you almost sound British. How long have you been down here?"

"Too long," she replies with her throat and eyes.

"Are you all right?" he repeats, his voice soft, like air in a village after a windstorm.

"Yes, I am now," she replies. "I had malaria. No big deal." She wants to fold herself into his arms, but she stands stiff and proud. "You should have seen the other guy." She smiles, but his eyes stay serious.

"Sexy," he says in a low murmur. "Your voice always has that power over me." He leans in, as close as business politesse will allow. "Dianna, will you have a drink with me tonight?" he asks. "To catch up?"

She looks into his eyes, ready to decline. He's being much too forward.

"At the Norfolk?" he asks again. "I'm at the Intercontinental."

"Yes," she says as simply and sadly as he has said her name.

"Call me," he says, walking back toward his colleagues. Her heart sinks because she knows she will not be introduced.

CHAPTER SEVEN: UNDER THE BRIDGE

May 31, 1991
The Norfolk Hotel
Nairobi, Kenya

The Norfolk Hotel is a gleaming colonial oasis carved out of dusty, urban grime. Dianna arrives first, of course. The maître d' attempts to seat her at a table for dinner, and he frowns when she tells him she is simply there for drinks. He leads her to a table overlooking the garden. The restaurant is open air, with lights twinkling everywhere, its very own festivity. A couple leans over a nearby table munching after-dinner chocolate truffles. The atmosphere is one of refined joviality, without any sign of the raucous underbelly seething to break free that Dianna is used to in Sudan. She leans back, incredulous that four days ago, she was in a rusting hospital bed, and a few weeks before that, she was in a feeding center that had no food.

She has become accustomed to waiting, so it is not as abhorrent to her as it was a decade ago. In fact, she finds it nice to rest and take in the melodious sounds of the night. Beyond this sophisticated scene, somewhere in this navy purple night, she can hear the quaver of the weaver birds and the shriller call of an ibis. Somewhere, a sleepy beast of burden, a mule perhaps, lows. If she tilts her head, she thinks she may hear a drumbeat, something so low and calm that she cannot tell if it is a human sound or an animal call. She takes in the scent of jasmine, euphorbia trees, and some herbal smell she cannot name, curry before it becomes curry.

When he enters, she is still lost in the moment, looking out into the night. How much time has passed? The glint of his cufflinks catches her eye, the ones she gave him long ago. She smiles in memory while wondering why he would still wear them. She wills herself not to read anything into it. She mentally lists what has changed and what has not. His hair is grayer, a bit thinner than the mane he once had. He is dark from the sun. His wrinkles are the same, a bit deeper, no more. He says something to the maître d,' and then he sees her. She stands to greet him.

Qasim advances to the table, almost gliding, in that way he has that is not quite of this world, not even of this equatorial twilight world, and clutches her wrists. He grins, broad and wide, and his lips catch hers despite her attempt to turn her head toward his cheek. The taste of his lips is salt and cologne and spicy skin. Their eyes meet, but then he looks down quickly, rubbing the tablecloth with his perfect nails. When he looks up again, his eyes have that old sarcastic, impish dance to them.

"I told you you'd never get rid of me," he whispers. He pulls her chair out, then goes to his seat and orders his Scotch and her wine. "I don't remember your hair being so blonde," he remarks, pushing a strand behind her ear. "Are you coloring it?"

She rolls her eyes. Same old Qasim. "No, the sun."

He does not hesitate, no embarrassment at all there. "Tell me, Dianna," he says.

She knows this phrase well. He always wanted to hear her stories, no matter how mundane. And now, she has something to say, and so she begins. She tells him about her time in Nairobi, her short time back in the U.S., her return trip to Addis. She even mentions her mother, her sister, her brother. Then she launches into Sudan, Biel, and Khalil. "Khalil reminds me of my brother at that age," she says, and she hears her voice quaver.

He grips her hand the entire time, but when she finishes, he leans back and drops it. She cannot tell if he is sad or deep in thought. Finally, he speaks.

"Dianna, there is nothing to be done for that child. He is caught. Don't let him pull you in with him."

"Qasim, I don't have to be pulled down with him. I can pull him out with me."

"No, Dianna. No. There's too much at stake. You must continue your year's contract. You must look this man in the eye every day. For heaven's sake, he is a warlord! I'm certain that he suspects your intentions. You may have already gone too far."

Dianna feels the anger surge up inside her and spill into her veins. "You are not there, Qasim. I am. I know what the boundaries are."

He looks at her with what might be contempt, and her heart beats faster. She did not mean for the conversation to take this wrong turn.

"Please, Qasim, let's get off this subject." She motions to the server and orders two more drinks. Qasim orders their dinner.

He takes a gulp from his Scotch glass and then a deep breath. "I travel tomorrow," he says. "I have to deal with some family business in Beirut."

"Are you okay?" Dianna asks. It is her turn to worry about him. Her mind drifts back to the first time they met in that smoky hall of mirrors. She wonders whether that was the illusion or if this is. Where is she heading, attempting to get a Sudanese out of Africa? Does she think she could actually be a single mother when she isn't even very good at being a daughter? All of a sudden, she wants to escape. She wants him to ask her to come with him.

His gaze penetrates hers; then, he looks down at her hands. "You're wearing that ring," he says.

"And you're wearing those cufflinks," she says by way of answer. "I want to know how you are," she repeats after a pause. Is he trying to change the subject or just trying to find the words?

The food arrives. The Norfolk's soup is famous, but she barely tastes it. She picks at her entrée, and so does he.

"It is difficult," he says, "losing both parents."

"Yes, your mother died long ago," she says. "I can only imagine how one continues. I still have my mother, at least a small part of her."

"Be thankful for her, Dianna," he says. "We never know how long we will be here, none of us." His eyes redden, and she does not know how to respond. "I don't have much hope for Lebanon," he says. "It is getting difficult to know what its future is. And where Beirut goes, I am afraid the rest of the region will follow."

"You, Qasim? Qasim, the optimist? Qasim, the fixer of all the world's problems?" She smiles, half proud, half cajoling.

"How much longer can this go on?" is all he says. Then, "After this assignment, I'm taking some time off to travel on my own again. I am ready to slow down—a little."

She wants to say, "Take me with you." Instead, she says, "Where will you go?"

"I have always wanted to see the Orient," he says.

She laughs at this Old-World euphemism, but she does not call him on it. The word brings images of elephant caravans, teas, and exotic spices. Funny, she wonders, is this what seems exotic to Qasim? Asia? India? She wonders if he has someone to accompany him, whom he will meet on the way.

"Have a wonderful time," she says and touches the smooth hair on the back of his hand. "I know how much you love a good journey." Finally, she plucks up her courage to ask, "Are you with someone now?"

"No." He laughs. "Still divorced. You?" He raises his eyebrows, and she can see what he looked like as a small boy.

"Of course not," she says. "In this place?"

"Lots of romances take off here," he says. "If you can take time off work." He shifts in his chair as though shifting thoughts. "I will call you when I return," he says, and this time, her laughter is louder. People gaze over at their table.

"Qasim, I have no telephone."

"Right," he says. He fumbles in his pocket, extracts some cards, squints in the dim light, shuffles them around, and finally hands her one. "Then here—here is my telephone number. I don't know how long I will be at this office, but they might know where to find me. If you ever need me . . ." His voice trails off.

"I'll do my best to call," she says, not knowing if she means it, not knowing what the next week, much less the next month, will bring. She glances at the card in English, French, and Arabic, then stashes it in her purse. Her heart beats a rat-a-tat-tat in her chest. She does not want him to get up and leave. Yet, she is terrified to look at him. He reaches under the table and grabs her knee with an urgency that jars her.

"Promise," he says.

"Yes, okay, I promise," she says, but her gaze remains fixed on the floor. A mosquito buzzes by her sandal, and she is catapulted back to Africa. She must deal with this continent, not some old ember of a flame.

She still does not have faith in his words.

They rise from the table. The mountain air is getting a chill to it, and he helps her on with her sweater. They walk out into the dusty night. Dianna catches sight of some sort of animal creeping into a crevice between two buildings. She's heard the rumors of hyenas roaming Nairobi at night, although she has never seen one. A pack of hyenas can tear a human apart. She catches Qasim's hand. "What was that?" she asks.

He peers into the darkness. "I see nothing," he says. "Look," he continues, and at first, she thinks he means to look at their surroundings. Then she notices he is looking at her and not across the street. "Look," he repeats. "Dianna, come with me."

Her heart lurches, and she steps off the dusty curb into the street. Does he mean come with him to East Asia or to Lebanon? The "y" of "yes" sticks in her throat like a seed. She struggles to get it out. "Okay," is all she can muster.

His eyes are full of light, and he grabs the hand with the ring on it. "Come on, then." He laughs. "What are we waiting for?"

Dianna pulls back and fishes for an excuse. "Qasim, I must pack."

"What do you need to pack for?" He frowns. "Are you leaving tomorrow?"

She knows now why she struggled with an affirmative answer to his invitation. Her intuition had known he did not mean East Asia or Lebanon. He meant his hotel room. She wishes she could live in the moment like he does, wanting only what he can get on a given date, in each place, the dates and places and people changing like the numbers on a digital stopwatch.

"No, Qasim, I am not leaving tomorrow, and I doubt I'll leave before I get someone to give me an answer about the little Sudanese boy. I can't come with you right now, though, because I can't . . . I won't sleep with you." She thinks about how much she wants to, remembers the last time they were together in a bed, and the night dances crazy, mocking, around her. "No, I cannot," she repeats. "Don't try again." To be with him again only to watch him leave would destroy her.

"You just told me you were coming with me." Qasim's frown deepens, and he tries to put his arm around her. She shrugs it off. His face gets ruddy, and he looks around as though someone has seen her public rebuff. She sees a taxi far away and puts up her hand to flag it down. It turns a corner and fades from view.

Maybe she is over him, maybe she is better off without him, but how does one forget a love, any love?

"Dianna, you must understand. I could not commit to you back then. It wasn't the right time or place." He grabs at her hand.

She pulls it away. "Qasim, that's water under the bridge. I don't want to talk about it. We've already been there, and we can't go back. It's too late for us."

"What bridge, my Dianna? Are bridges not made to join and unite, not divide?" He laughs, and she gives him a frown, though she's not angry, only frustrated that he either doesn't understand what she wants her words to convey, or he's back in a patronizing role. He takes both her hands in his, and this time, she lets him. "I had nothing to give you then, Dianna. I do now." He looks earnest enough, but his eyes move back and forth in the shadows. She has seen that look before from him, and now, from others, elsewhere in Africa, when someone is not sharing the entire truth.

"I want more than a night, Qasim," she replies. "I may have nothing to give you now, myself, after all this time. I've had to move on. I assumed you had as well. Maybe we're just too different." She looks up into the sky to hold her tears back, and finds a shooting star, not uncommon in these sapphire-sky, equatorial nights. It dances, streaks, and then disappears. A tear trickles down her cheek, then another.

"Nonsense!" His voice soars with conviction. "You will never get rid of me, Dianna," he says, and his eyes bore into hers like a chemical liquid.

He may well be telling a sad truth. She believes him, but she wants to be by his side, not just in his arms for a night. He flits in and out of her life like a slender switch, baiting her. "I have an early day tomorrow. I can't come with you, and that's final."

His lips get completely and absolutely straight, and then they begin to tremble. "I stayed an extra night to see you," he says.

She makes her heart cold and hard like her frigid floor in Sudan. She does not know what it would take to expand it. When it slips out of hiding for a moment . . . for Khalil . . . for Qasim . . . it only knows pain. To get hurt again. To get rejected again. She cannot give Qasim any small portion of herself; each meeting puts another tiny nick in her veins. She puts up her arm to flag a cab again.

An old black British-style hulk of a cab pulls up alongside them. Qasim opens the door for her, and she turns to get in. "Promise you'll call me," he says and pulls her to him and gives her a long, deep kiss, which she submits to, at first as a small token for memories past, then as something to hold onto to get her through the future.

"Promise," she answers. The kiss has affected her, and this time, she means what she says. What harm could come from a telephone conversation?

When she looks back as the cab drives away, he is standing there, his hands in his pockets, watching. Her heart is still small, but it has melted a bit tonight. The memories are beginning to pry open the box she has locked them in. She thinks this might be the last time she ever sees him again, and she waves like a frantic child. She cannot tell if he sees her. Then the African night envelops him, and he is gone.

CHAPTER EIGHT: FLIGHT

June 1, 1991
Nairobi, Kenya

The next morning dawns early, and she makes her way through the business district. The old railroad terminus is still there, a reminder of bygone colonial days. Presently, bereft of purpose, the building sits— passed by—its bricks and mortar crumbling in silent testimony to a once-beguiling, now extinct era. She notices but doesn't worry about some fighter jets circling the city above her. A few fighters in the sky no longer faze her.

What does faze her are the stares from people on the street. She is wearing a bright sundress, carefully hemmed below the knee. A worker at the hospital retrieved it from the dust bin, laundered it, and gave it to her. She certainly couldn't wear the soiled clothes she'd arrived in. Perhaps its cut or polka dots are causing the stares. She holds her satchel closer to her body and trudges on, with purpose, a city-cultivated skill. *Why are they staring?* Better this than jeans or a piece of kitenge cloth for an important embassy visit.

She endures the long wait in the vestibule, looking at the photos of diplomats on every wall. She thinks back to explaining "boredom" to Khalil and chuckles to herself. She wishes she had a book to read. She takes out the embassy man's card to make sure she remembers his name. She crosses and uncrosses her legs, making sure her skirt covers her knees for modesty's sake. Her foot is tapping on the tile when the man she spoke with yesterday approaches her.

He extends his hand and apologizes. "Sorry, Miss Calloway. We've had some unexpected business come up. I've made a few calls and come up with nothing. I wish we could help. Really, I do. However, there is no way for you to take a minor out of that country without beginning formal adoption proceedings, and there is no way that you can do that for Sudanese children, especially conscripted Sudanese children."

"But Mr. Davis, this is a baby we are talking about!" Dianna stomps her foot and takes a step toward him.

He steps back and puts his palms out. "You must listen to me, Miss Calloway . . . Dianna. For your safety, and for diplomatic relations, for your work in the Sudan." He smiles a weak wire of a smile and extends a hand again.

Dianna does not take it. "I have no idea what you think you're doing in Africa, Mr. Davis, if you do not even attempt to save babies from war, but this is one step further than war. This could be pedophilia!" She stomps again. "A free democracy cannot stand for this!"

The man sniggers. Then he begins to laugh outright. She fails to see any humor in this situation. He seems off balance, like he is laughing hysterically about something completely aside from the topic. She stands stiff and straight and stares him down.

He begins to calm down. "Miss Calloway, pedophiles exist everywhere: in dictatorships as well as democracies, in peaceful countries, and especially in war-torn ones. I empathize with your desire to save this child, but we must all consider the greater good. I am sure that Dr. Biel would hate to let you go. You seem a competent-enough teacher."

Dianna takes this as a veiled threat. This time, she does not stomp, but her face burns, and her fingers tremble. She points at him. "I assure you, Mr. Davis . . . Edwin, that I will not let this go." She whips around and heads toward the door. She pushes it open with a whoosh and coughs at the dust that accosts her. Outside, the wind has whipped up, and she can barely see in front of her. She hears helicopter blades overhead. She feels an arm take her elbow, and startled, she jerks it away.

"Come on, Dianna, let me take you to the airport," Qasim says with a steadiness that frightens her.

"Were you here all along?" she asks, but he does not answer. He steers her away from the embassy building, toward the intersection, and this time, he flags a cab. She notices he clutches a suitcase in his other hand.

"Why are you here?" she asks, hoping this time for a response. He says nothing else until they are in the taxi.

"I am taking you to the airport." He looks over his shoulder and then up into the rearview mirror.

"What's wrong?" she asks.

"Nothing. Just that a car is following us too closely."

She wants to ask him how long he has been here since he is so unfamiliar with Nairobi drivers, but she is too perplexed to venture any sort of humor. She has never seen him looking this serious.

"Why did you pick me up?" she asks, her voice low so that only he can hear.

"Do you have luggage?" he asks her, and she shakes her head no.

She already carries her only satchel containing a few pieces of clothing, a bar of soap, and a toothbrush she bought here this week. And, of course, her perpetual bottle of water. Emergency medical evacuations do not allow time to gather one's belongings. Her belongings have little meaning to her anyway, aside from a few mementos back at camp, one of which he gave her.

He smiles and pushes her hair behind her ear, just as he did the night before. "It was so good to see you. You look beautiful today, really. You do."

"Why are you here, Qasim? My plane doesn't leave for hours."

"There has been a bomb threat. They are uncertain whom it's targeting. You heard the planes? They were heading to patrol the Ugandan border. There's been some sort of skirmish there. It's better if you get to the airport. No telling if the threat is real."

Dianna rolls her eyes. "There are bomb threats all the time! Is that all this is? Or are you trying to manipulate me into . . ." Qasim takes her wrist in his hand so tightly that it hurts her. She grimaces in pain. "Stop that!" she cries, and he releases her.

"Dianna, you still have a lot to learn," he says. "Do you know who owns the Norfolk?" He smiles, but his eyes droop when she shakes her head no. "It is a favorite British haunt; Americans like it almost as much as the Thorn Tree, and it is owned by Israelis. Did you know it was bombed?"

She stares, baffled.

"Oh yes, a decade ago. Do you know why?"

Dianna opens her mouth but says nothing. She vaguely recognizes Nairobi flashing by like movie footage through her cracked window.

"In 1976, Kenya offered support to an Israeli commando team on a hostage-rescue mission in Uganda," he says, looking out the window instead of at her. "A Palestinian militia group hijacked an Air France jet there. In 1980, fifteen people were killed in the Norfolk by terrorists. Idi Amin never forgave Kenya for its intervention. He believes Kenya colluded with Israel. The world thinks things are calming down now that the Cold War is over. Yet, the world is a pendulum. A force cannot stop moving one way without eventually moving the other."

He pauses as though rethinking what he planned to say.

"Maybe today, nothing will happen. Let us hope and pray. Yet, that was what those fifteen people were thinking on New Year's Eve 1980. Better safe than sorry. Westerners in bright sundresses are targets here, whether they realize it or not." He looks at her, and his eyes convince her he might be right.

Yet, still again, Dianna says nothing. There is nothing to say. She half believes he has saved her from something tragic, and she's certain he believes he has.

"Sorry I hurt you," he adds, massaging her wrist. "Did I really hurt you?"

Dianna takes her wrist away. "Yes," she says. Then louder, "Yes."

"I wanted to get you away from here," he says, "before you got yourself into real trouble, one way or another. After that, my dear, you are on your own." He takes out a starched white handkerchief and wipes his forehead. "My, the air is full of dust and heat today."

This is the old Qasim, full of attentiveness and overprotection, full of affection and irritation, all at once. Dianna clutches her hands in her lap, and when she looks up, she can feel the gratitude showing in her gaze. "Thank you, Qasim," she says. "Thank you, whether it was justified or not, for saving me from myself."

He laughs. "You do get yourself in the biggest binds."

Dianna giggles back. "You're one to talk. Truce?" She shakes her wrist to erase the ache, then extends her hand to him.

"Truce!" They hold hands the rest of the way to the airport.

● ● ●

"Let me buy you some water," he says when they arrive at the airport.

As they stand in line together at the cashier, she teases him about Nairobi's lack of bottled water. "Where's the Perrier you told me about on my first trip to Africa?" She grins. He'd told her she'd have no trouble finding clean water in any Intercontinental, as if the U.N. put their workers on the ground up in fancy hotels.

Qasim looks crestfallen and a bit bewildered. "Didn't you check out the shop at the Intercontinental?" he asks with a sheepish grin. "They have Perrier."

Dianna decides to leave the conversation there. She does not tell him she has never seen the inside of the Intercontinental. She suspects he has not had to deal with bartering for a fifty-year-old Coke bottle rolled in the dirt or to drink water that tastes like bleach and is buzzing with flies.

Qasim must rush to catch his plane when they arrive at the terminal. He squeezes her hand, gives her a kiss, and hugs her tight. "I'm looking forward to your call when you leave Sudan," he says.

"How long will you be gone yourself?" she asks.

"Three or four months. I'm due for some time off to wrap up my father's estate. I haven't had a vacation in a few years." He brushes a piece of lint off his jacket sleeve and adjusts his tie. How can a man stay in a suit on such a hot day?

"Is that all you're taking?" she asks.

"I travel light, just like you."

"Stay safe." She touches his chin.

"I should be the one telling you that."

"Promise me you'll stay safe," she says, her hand caressing his lapel.

She doesn't want him to go, but what choice do they have? It didn't work the first time; why should it work now? And where would it work? It hurts, just like leaving home. No. It hurts more than leaving home.

"So long," she tells him, using the phrase her uncle used. He never told anyone goodbye after World War II. It was always 'so long.' She wonders how long it will be this time.

"So long," Qasim says, and his words sound foreign and familiar at the same time.

She watches him walk up the tarmac. Miraculously, his plane is there already. When did a plane ever leave on time in Nairobi? He still floats through the air, his feet gliding over the pavement. He turns, blows her a kiss, and mouths, "Promise."

She waves him out of sight, and somehow, her farewell this time seems right. Then she turns, updates her ticket, and walks back to the boarding area. In one corner, some men in somber polyester suits smoke cigarettes and drink tea in cracked white cups. In another, a mother dressed in loose, comfortable, bright rainbow colors and uncomfortable-looking high-heeled sandals nurses twins. In still another, a Masai warrior, dressed in royal blood-red from high cheek bones to long toes, grasps a carved walking stick and sends her a meditative gaze. Everywhere, noise bounces off the walls of this self-described "state of the art" international airport. She spends a few Kenyan shillings on gum, another water bottle, and postcards for her family. Her brother will enjoy the new stamps. Then she sighs and turns in the few remaining shillings that are mandatory upon leaving the country.

So long, Qasim. So long, Kenya.

The speaker comes on. "Ladies and Gentleman," a proper Kenyan voice announces. "Flight 345 to Khartoum has been delayed. We apologize for the inconvenience."

"Probably that bomb that delayed traffic," a woman behind her says. "It must have gone off."

Dianna sits down, prepared for a long wait. *So, it was real.*

How could so much have happened in a few weeks? Sudan seems a million miles and lifetimes away. Her heart is no longer fully in it. Sickness has taken something out of her, and Qasim has reminded her she's not as strong as she believes. Her stomach flip-flops as she thinks about the long plane ride ahead to Sudan and Biel. And Khalil. She wonders what else waits for her there.

CHAPTER NINE: DESCENT

June 3, 1991
Juba, Southern Sudan

"You had a safe flight?" Driver asks, helping her into the car, looking around for luggage but finding none. She knows she can't delay, but so far, there's no evidence of bombing here. Not even war. She's nonetheless grateful to have made it back alive.

"Yes," she says with a simple fondness. Qasim may have saved her from tragedy in Kenya, but she presumes she has Driver to thank for saving her from cerebral malaria. She can't ask him what he did—because his life, and probably his family's, is tied to Biel. He'd never admit any role he'd played in putting her in danger or for keeping her safe and alive because he likes her. It's a balancing act played on a lit match. She has to play her role as much as he does. She will miss Driver when she leaves this Sudanese assignment, which may be sooner than later at the rate she's going.

"You lived in Africa for a while before you came to Sudan," Driver states as they round the bend and head from the airfield toward the camp.

"Yes," she says, wondering what comes next. "I've been in Kenya, Zaire, and Ethiopia. Why?"

"You have treated me like a person since you got here. Some of us you like, and others you do not like." He looks in the rearview mirror; it seems to ascertain her reaction.

Her trip to Nairobi changed her; Qasim is still on her mind. "Ummm," is all she answers. She is thinking about how some Western *khawajas* treat Africans. Some treat them as if it is a kill-or-be-killed situation. Some treat them as manipulative children who need a good thrashing. Still others ignore them entirely, as though they do not exist. Even so, she's amused and embarrassed that this comment comes from a man she simply knows as Driver, whose real name she does not even know, although not for lack of trying. Why won't he tell her his name?

She stiffens as they get closer to camp. Until now, she was caught in an emotional valley, dividing her feeling of safety during her ride to the airport with Qasim and the dread that engulfs her the closer she gets to Biel. Rain pelts the closed window, and Driver has had to get out and push the vehicle out of ruts twice. Dianna has gotten out, too, exercising politeness but knowing she lacks the strength right now to help him.

"The southwesterlies have arrived this year after many dry seasons," he remarks. "It may be inconvenient, but it will help our people in the long run. No more famine."

Dianna sends up a silent prayer of thanks for at least something that has gone right in this country. She wonders if the "people" have had time amid fighting and fleeing to cultivate anything for the rain to nourish. She sees only barren fields on either side of the road as she and Driver advance further from the hills, deeper into the South. Every so often, an irrigated cotton field prospers, but farmers are usually not there to attend or pick. They can't eat cotton anyway. The conflict has been going on for years; no one can really tell her for certain when it started. The layers pile one upon the other and divide endlessly, like amoebas: North versus South, Muslim versus Christian, with sectarian divisions within, Arab versus Nilotic, with tribal divisions within, Colonial versus African. Add the icing on this multi-layer sheet cake that is Sudan—its language differences, economic disputes, racial prejudices, slavery—and the list of grievances capable of resulting in violence seems nearly endless, like a star that has just imploded, making its own lethal universe.

"Driver, do you have family?" she asks.

"Yes, I have many children, but they are far away," he answers.

Two birds of prey fly overhead, circling some lunch in the bottom of a gorge beneath them. "I hear it is sacrilege for the Nuer tribe to kill birds." She watches the birds' circle grow bigger and then smaller, then bigger again.

"Yes," he says. "Animals are important to us, and the birds are close to God. Some think it is only the Nuer who revere the animals, but the Dinka tribe does as well. As do the smaller tribes. We cannot live without the animals. That is why we have blood vengeance for cattle raids. Yet, we humans are the highest of the animals, the Dinka and the Nuer, the Arabs and us, the Muslims and the Christians. God created us. We are as sacred as the birds. I do wish that we would realize our sanctity as we do the birds' and the cattle's."

Dianna is silent in the face of his wisdom until they roll into camp. When she gets out of the back seat, she bows in respect to the older man. He returns the bow and restarts the engine, which starts, stalls, and starts again. He leaves in a cloud of mud and dust, and Dianna is once again left alone.

She doesn't know whether to try to find food and water, to go to her housing to rest before confronting Biel, or to search for Khalil. She decides to go to her dwelling before anyone knows she has returned. She stands in the doorway, letting her eyes adjust to the darkness inside. When she can finally see, she lets out a little gasp. Her belongings have been pillaged. Her bedding has been ripped, and feathers still float through the air from her one thin mattress, now in shreds. Her trunk is broken at the hinges, and the suitcase has been thrown in a corner, its lock forced open. Her few changes of clothes that weren't sent with her are caked with grime and insects.

Dianna looks frantically for the three things that are meaningful to her, other than the plain jewelry she wears. Her gratitude knows no bounds that she was wearing her green onyx university ring when she became ill. Her journal is nowhere to be found, nor is the chain with the Claddagh ring from her old friend Connor. The mosaic box from Qasim rests on its side in the far corner. Its hinge is torn, its red felt lining ripped, but it is still there. Her fingers move as they would over Braille, determining the damage. Only two pieces of mosaic are missing.

Tears flow freely as she lifts the box and works the hinge. It is easily repaired. The lining is a different matter. She will need to search for a similar fabric. She runs her finger over the inside to see if it was glued or stapled on. As she does, her finger finds a piece of yellowed paper, the one thing the thieves, informants, or militants missed in her otherwise destroyed abode. It has been under the lining all this time. She lifts it up like a scroll. It is folded six ways. Her fingers fumble with each fold until she can finally read the inscription, which is in Arabic. In Qasim's handwriting.

Outside, she approaches the first man that comes her way. She knows his face, but she does not know his name. "Excuse me," she says louder than she intended. "I've returned, but someone has destroyed my home."

The man looks past her to her doorway and shakes his head. He does not say anything for a long time. Then he says, "Dr. Biel is in his quarters. He will want to know you are here."

Dianna wants to ask him the meaning of the Arabic, but he may not even read the Nuer language. Nor does he seem the person to comprehend what this message from the past might say. She mentally slaps herself; it may not be a message. It may simply be a note of quality the manufacturer put there. Yet the box does not seem mass-produced. Perhaps it is an artisan's signature. She races to Biel's hut.

He is poring over some sort of map; it seems to be a map of Germany or Eastern Europe, not of Sudan or Africa. She pauses to subdue her anxiety. "Excuse me," she says, as calmly as she can muster. "I wanted to thank you for getting me to the clinic in Nairobi. Was it all on your order that my home was destroyed?"

"Why would I care one way or another about your home? My men tend to the camp. You were away."

"I was only away because of you." Her breath comes out hot, enunciating every word.

"I did not make you ill, Miss Calloway."

She wants to pummel his chest, rant, shout. "You had something to do with it, and you know it!"

"Only God above can make man healthy, make man ill," he says without a change in expression. "How could I, a healthy man, make you ill? And why would I destroy your little . . . souvenirs?" His lip upturns just a millimeter.

They stare each other down.

"Why are you here?" he says at last.

"You may have no more use for me here, but I wanted to be able to see you in person. I also came to claim my belongings, but this box is all that's left." She holds the box up for his inspection. She would have shoved it in his face, but she doesn't want him to touch it. Destroy one of the last things that means anything to her, like he destroyed her other belongings, like he destroyed her heart by separating her from Khalil.

"Damascene," he mutters.

"Yes," she says. "It was a gift that I treasured."

Biel rubs his chin as though he does not know how to respond. "Yes," he finally says. "I have lost many treasures. My son, for one."

Dianna's throat closes over. "I am sorry," she says. "I didn't know."

"It was a long time ago," he says and starts to read the map again.

The box and his confession have made the topic of Khalil one she must defer until she asks about the Arabic phrase she holds, or until she can find someone else who can translate it. She holds it up so that it catches the light that shines from Biel's lantern. "I was wondering if you could translate this for me," she requests. "You read a little Arabic?"

"Yes, I know Arabic," he says. "What is it? Let me see it."

She holds it out to him, not stepping further into his hut. "Something I found," she mumbles.

Biel looks at the paper, folds it, and unfolds it. He rubs his chin, then grins. "Where did you find this?"

"It's mine," Dianna says, not willing to budge. "From many years ago."

"I should hope so," Biel says with his slow, sly grace.

"What does it say?" Dianna asks again.

"You understand that Arabic is a language of words that build upon one another?" he questions.

Dianna does not know this fact, but she nods her head anyway.

"Not just a word, but a set of consonants that start as one word, then add three more and a vowel, and it becomes another, and so on?" Dianna is beginning to understand as he continues. "You've heard that Eskimos have a certain number of words for 'snow' and that Egyptians have a certain number of words for 'sand.' Language invents many words for something it has a plentitude of."

Dianna furrows her brow; she's afraid he has lost her. What do snow and sand have to do with what's on the paper he holds? Why can't he just give her the direct translation, for God's sake? This man despises her as much as she does him.

Then she realizes he's taking his time because he's toying with her.

His eyes pierce through her. "Arabic has many words for 'love.'"

• • •

Foolish of her to give it to him to read. She snatches the piece of paper and turns abruptly to go, her shoes crunching beneath her on his dirt floor.

"Miss Calloway?" he calls after her, his snide laughter bouncing toward her. "Don't you want to know which one it was?"

Biel's voice is still ringing in her ears as she races to her room and pushes all the mud and cloth she can salvage into a plastic bag with Qasim's box at the bottom. She carefully folds the message and puts it in her pocket. *Qasim had loved her.* She wants out, and she wants out now, but first, she must find Khalil. She does not know whether it will be to take him with her or say goodbye. She slings her bag over her shoulder and searches every nook and cranny of the camp.

Khalil is nowhere to be found. The sun shines high in the sky; it scorches her shoulders, and then it is low again. The other boys have returned from their duty and training. They follow her around, asking for cigarettes. She is angry at them all; who knows which one of them helped trash her belongings? She refuses to imagine that it was someone more sinister than these boys, looking for candy and cigs.

She sits down under one of the few shade trees in the camp and sobs, big, grieving gulps from so deep in her body she wonders if it has a name. The boys pat her cheeks and make clucking sounds for a long time. Then they hear the supper bell and disappear.

When Dianna looks up again, she can hear the night insects, a big whirring sound, with an occasional chirp breaking the sound of the entomological machine. The biggest moon she has ever seen is beginning to rise. Biel stands at her feet.

"Rude of you to run away from our meeting." The moonlight reveals a sneer as sinister as the moon is full. "Your services are no longer needed here. I have called a ride for you," he says. "It will take you to the airport tomorrow morning."

"Where is Khalil?" she spits out at him. Silent tears still stain her neck.

"I have told you. He is none of your business. You should not have interfered. Your interference has caused him to be sent away." His eyes narrow. "Far away."

Her mind is racing with places he could have sent him. His face gives nothing away.

"Is he alive?" she asks.

"I wish you the best elsewhere." He grimaces, then extends his hand. She does not return his gesture. "By the way," he says, reaching into his pocket and handing her a telegram, never taking his eyes off her face. "This came while you were incapacitated."

It is another folded message, and Dianna unfolds it, watching Biel's steely face. Mama had stroke STOP Still alive for now STOP You need to come STOP T.C. quit his job STOP Come home STOP Mary Ann STOP

CHAPTER TEN:
DEBRIEF

June 4, 1991
Southern Sudan Delegation
Juba, Southern Sudan

She feels like a branded soldier or defrocked nun, but if Dianna turns in her ID badge, they might someday let her back in this country. Mirembe is at the counter going through her file. Not surprising to have a woman there to debrief her. They're probably hoping she'll open up and tell them something they don't know.

Surprisingly, Mirembe doesn't ask many questions. Probably because she's working more for the tribe than the U.N. If she'd known this earlier, she could have played her loyalty to Biel to her better advantage. How deep do their loyalties go?

Mirembe motions her to set down her luggage, and they kiss on both cheeks, then a third time, like the Swiss do. They almost bump noses, and they both laugh. Nervous laughter.

"Won't you come have some tea with me?" Mirembe asks, and Dianna agrees. The more liquid she drinks before her dehydrating flights back to the U.S., the better. She sinks into a chair with a sagging seat. A huge mosquito languishes on the windowsill. She feels as much hope as that mosquito must feel. Bring on the inquisition.

She hands Mirembe her badge and tells her that the supplies left at camp are minimal. Explains she'd arrived back from Nairobi to a vandalized dwelling. She does not mention the few things she saved. That would lead to further inquiry. It may get back to Biel. It's none of Mirembe's business anyway. She still has a spark of desire to return for Khalil, but she won't let Mirembe know that.

She doubts she'll ever be back.

That's why Mirembe's next words shock her. "I hope you return."

Dianna can feel her face warm. "Really?"

"Yes, very much. It was pleasant having you around."

"I am sorry to leave. If it weren't for my mother's illness, I would not. I would fight to stay. I feel horrible that I did not fulfill my mission." Dianna's voice breaks. So much sadness. So much grief.

"It was an incredibly difficult mission. I am sorry to see you go, saddened by how the boys mistreated you."

"The boys?"

"Your students." She offers Dianna a chair and sits in her seat.

"My students. I just hope they learned something from me," Dianna says. "I thought the little one, Khalil, had a chance, but he seems to have been sent away from camp."

Mirembe's thick brows arch. "Khalil is no longer there?"

"No, at least not that I could see."

Mirembe's smile fades. She's troubled Mirembe, but she can't ascertain why.

"I will need to discover why," Mirembe says. "You have no idea?"

"No. None."

"He was learning well, though?"

"Until Biel asked me to stop teaching him."

"Oh." Mirembe's hands tighten in her lap. "I am surprised by that."

"Why?"

"I would think he would want Khalil educated. I agree Khalil should be with Biel, but it is a complicated situation. Biel is a warrior, yes, but he may be Khalil's father."

"What? You mean—"

Ted walks in at the wrong time and slaps Dianna's back. "Time to move out, old girl."

Dianna obliges. She wants more information, but it's best to leave before anyone can question her further. If she couldn't get help for Khalil in Nairobi, she certainly can't here.

"Thank you both." Dianna extends a hand, but they both give her light hugs. "For the opportunity, the learning experience," she finishes with some difficulty. She will not weep in front of them. She turns one last time to Mirembe. "Please," she says, wondering if she is going too far but doing it anyway, "please, if you find out where Khalil is, will you let me know?" She scribbles her mother's address, the only one she's got at present. "You can always find me here."

"Of course, my dear," Mirembe says. "I know we shall miss you. May I keep in touch then?"

Even if Mirembe wants her in Africa, Biel will do everything to keep her out. Mirembe's ties are here, but she yearns for that connection, however distant.

"By all means." She walks out into a world that doesn't want her. She's on her way to another that may want her even less.

CHAPTER ELEVEN:
AMNESTY

June 10, 1991
Richfield, North Carolina

The Piggly Wiggly is hopping. Dianna doesn't recall it ever being this busy on a weekday morning. Why isn't everyone at work? Where did all these people come from? This used to be a small town.

White noise whirs all around as she strolls up and down the aisles in shopping catatonia. She's never noticed the humming before; it must come from the refrigeration units. The cool air from the freezers whips at her cheeks, just as the hot wind whipped only a few days ago in Africa. She gawks at the variety of children's cereals, potato chips, and some new cookies bearing the claim "new and fat-free!" How strange it would be to eat lots of cookies and not get fat. She hopes no one is thinking of sending fat-free cookies to Africa like they send wool sweaters.

She is in search of adult diapers. Her mother has been complaining because the nurses leave her undressed. Dianna has never searched for infant diapers, let alone adult ones. She has no idea what aisle they'd be on. Another American invention rural Africa would never see. At least not in her lifetime.

She stops a clerk to ask their whereabouts.

"Not me! I work in dairy!" A scowl spreads across her full face, exposing a missing tooth and swollen gum. That must be so painful! She goes for help elsewhere.

Dianna finally reaches the cleaning supplies aisle, and a fellow customer takes pity on her. "They're on aisle twenty-seven," he says and points over his head to the left.

Half the shelves are filled with adult diapers.

She closes her eyes, twirls her finger around, and grabs the first one she touches. Pin the finger on the diaper. How different from the market in Nairobi, so close, confining, and at first almost menacing, but then so warm. The five-and-dime of her childhood, the smell of stale popcorn, nail polish, and pencil lead. This grocery superstore is so—so clinical. Who would know anything in this store was cultivated in the ground or that animals sacrificed their lives for the sterile white packages in the meat section?

The checkout aisles have new do-it-yourself credit card transaction machines. You slide your card, punch a few buttons, and voila, your transaction is complete. Everyone else knows how to work them, but Dianna is a transaction machine virgin.

The elderly lady in line behind her begins to mutter. "Damn machines." This starts a conversation about fallible humans and infallible automation.

A middle-aged man in a neon green T-shirt asks no one in particular, "What happened to customer service?" Meanwhile, two more people join the five people already in line behind Dianna for their turn at the machine.

"Come on, ma'am," says a young man in a flannel shirt holding a six-pack under one arm. "Get a move on." His eyes track the diapers on the conveyer belt.

Dianna keeps sliding Mary Ann's debit card up and down, but the machine continues to flash "Transaction Void." She fishes in her pocket for the only American currency she owns . . . a ten-dollar bill. It is not there. Sweat pierces the back of her neck. The old lady begins to plunk her groceries on the conveyer belt, still mumbling. When Dianna inserts the card correctly on her fifth try, the lady mutters, "It's about time!"

Dianna whirls around. "Come on, lady! Give me a break!"

The old lady puts her hand to her heart. "My stars!"

Dianna hurls herself out of the grocery store, then realizes she is clutching the diapers but has left Mary Ann's debit card in the machine. She slinks back in to pick it up and gets back in line. The people in line turn and scowl at her; their silent reproach bounces between the candy counter and her mother's unwrapped diapers. She closes her eyes. Right now, the sun is setting on the African savannah, its maize-y gold crowning an iridescent purple. There, she feels calmer.

In time, she reaches the cashier again, who throws the debit card her way. It lands on the floor. Dianna picks it up and leaves with her head held high this time, returning the cashier's scorn. No matter, she is the proud and legal owner of a pack of "Pax" diapers, her booty stashed and invisible in a white plastic bag.

The engine of her sister Mary Ann's fifteen-year-old Chrysler doesn't turn on the first or second try, but it finally cooperates. She has to keep her foot on the accelerator at stop lights so it doesn't stall. People wave at her, and she waves back. They must know her; she is a Calloway, and this town is small, but she has no clue who they are. Perhaps they think she is Mary Ann. Or they're just Southern-Friendly. Too bad that doesn't apply to grocery lines any longer.

Tucked into a rocky hill, the hospital looks more jail than infirmary. She mounts the stairs to the intensive care unit past a newfangled cappuccino machine. She wishes she had the coins to try a cup, although the brew coming from a machine is probably more chemicals than coffee. A jet-lagged exhaustion is overtaking her, and it's only 10:00 a.m.

It is difficult to sit in this room watching her mother's long bony fingers and drawn mouth, playing out the possible outcomes. Where will she be next week and the week after? She dares not think about standing at the gaping hole that will be her mother's grave. She has seen too many open graves. She has no idea how they will pay for a funeral. She has no idea where her ten-dollar bill has gone, which was the last of her converted currency. She can't pay for a cup of coffee, let alone a funeral!

The beeps and whirs continue like a death mantra. Mary Ann comes in on her work break, and eventually, their brother T.C. sidles in, his hands in his pockets, leans his tall, lanky frame over, and gives Dianna a hug but leaves as quickly as he came.

"She's asleep. I'll be right back with some lunch," Mary Ann whispers, and the door whisks shut behind her.

Her mother stirs. "Clean me up, Dianna." Her mother's slurred speech floats across to her corner, where Dianna sits in her own little chair, just like Cinderella in the Rodgers and Hammerstein musical she used to watch on television once a year. Dianna's legs feel heavy. She fumbles to get the diapers out of the bag.

"Fine," Dianna answers. Antiseptic has spilled on the floor across the room, and a wire has detached from her mother's arm. She wipes up the spill but can't reattach the wire. She'll have to find a nurse to tell. The call button doesn't seem to work. Her mother will live or die, no matter how many wires she has sticking out of her body. How many things can they monitor at once?

The call button must work, after all. A nurse comes in to reattach the wire and then nods her head toward the hallway. "Can I see you outside for a moment?"

When they are outside the room, the woman's pervasive cheer fades.

Dianna pushes her hands into her jean skirt pockets and prepares for the bad news.

"The cardiologist wants to speak to you. He will be by after he finishes next door. Please wait here." The nurse hurries away like a gale of wind.

Dianna will never get rid of this memory of her mother in the hospital—the odor of bleach trying to cover up urine, blood, and pain. It's not that the mortal smells of Africa could be erased either. Yet, lingering didn't exist in the developing world. Dianna recalls seeing a frantic Dinka father racing with his dying son in his arms, back to their home and relative safety after an attack. The little boy had soiled his pants. For him, that one letting go of the body would be his last. How much suffering, she doesn't know. But rapid.

She'd expected her mother to keel over as her father did. For her death to be over in a blink. Yet, with her mother, it is day in and day out, scrape and crawl, inch by inch, to the end.

Dianna leans against the wall, feeling pale. She knows now what pale really means, and it doesn't mean lack of sun. It means fear so deep you're not sure where it began. She counts the options: She may be an orphan by the end of the week, a real orphan. She will be the one to handle the estate, or lack of one. She has no assignment and doubts Operation Ready to Read will keep her on after her experience in Sudan. She does not want to be here in this place that smells of slow death. She does not want to return to Africa, where death is quick and brutal, with no antiseptic smell, no pain meds.

Her mother's cardiologist is good-looking in a scientific sort of way, thick black hair brushed back on his head. He reminds her of her recent hospital stay and the handsome doctor who saved her life less than a couple of months ago. He echoes her posture by stuffing his hands in his pockets. He must be trying to make her comfortable. He moistens his lips before he speaks. "Your mother is a very, very ill woman."

"I realize this," Dianna says. Does he think she doesn't know, hasn't known for her entire life how ill her mother is? If only she had someone here to help her make these life-or-death decisions. Qasim? She'd been avoiding thinking about him, and she is miffed at herself because he's intruded . . . the memory, as vivid as the reality of this hospital corridor. Qasim waving at her, those last few moments at the Nairobi airport. Small comfort, but comfort nonetheless.

What did Qasim do when his mother was near death? Was he even there with her?

Mary Ann walks up the hallway with a measured gait, carrying two Caesar salads and a hot dog. "Oh, Dr. Kumar! It's nice to see you."

"If one thing doesn't get her, another will," Dr. Kumar continues, looking straight at Dianna. "The stroke, as you know, was caused by a blocked carotid artery. We've done tests and found the other carotid artery is blocked. We could go in and repair the artery, but I think not. This procedure . . ." He takes his hands out of his pockets. "It is quite risky for a woman in her condition."

He pauses again, looks at her as though he is assessing her strength.

"The problem is . . ." His hands go deeper into his pockets, and he pulls out a thermometer. He inspects it as though it will give him his next words. "The problem is, if we do nothing, she doesn't stand a chance. Her lungs are already shutting down. We'll have to use a respirator. Does your mother have a living will?"

Mary Ann lets out a sound like she is clearing her throat, but Dianna recognizes it as a choke. She used to make this sound years ago when she feared the dark. Dianna clutches Mary Ann's hand, and Mary Ann looks to Dianna for a decision. Mary Ann sways a bit, a half-confused, half-expectant look marring her tired brow.

Dianna doesn't even know exactly what a living will is. She thought Mary Ann was the one who would sign off on all this. She's the one living closest. But everyone is deferring to her now that she has returned, the Prodigal Sister. Every time she has taken on a new assignment, her family has argued it's time to come home, mend fences, help, and become more responsible. She's all but been vanquished since she left the U.S. As though she had no career or responsibilities in Africa. As though the only people on earth were these three people—her two younger siblings and her mother. It's strange to be deferred to after all these years. Stranger still to hold decisions about her mother's life in her hands.

The woman who once controlled Dianna's every movement, who tried to beat her into submission, is now relying on her decisions. The vulture that devoured her childhood has become a tiny, starving bird with a broken wing.

"Dr . . ." She's forgotten this doctor's name. He is one of a cadre of physicians who parade in and out of her mother's room, looking at her charts instead of her body. Her body is the nurse's job, and beyond that, everything else, Dianna's job. It's obvious her siblings have been waiting for her to make these final decisions. Maybe her mother has been holding on for her, too.

"Dr. Kumar." The man smiles at her, and she is touched by him showing his humanity. He brushes her arm with his hand. "I know this is difficult."

"Dr. Kumar," Dianna says again. "We will be all right if she dies. She's been ill my entire adult life. What is hard is the vigil. The not knowing. The suffering. *Her* suffering."

"Are you saying you want to proceed with the surgery?" His eyes are wide.

"How long does she have if we do nothing?"

"A few months, perhaps." His eyes soften.

"Then you must do what you must do."

"I ask again: Is this permission for the surgery?"

Mary Ann touches Dianna's arm and walks away. She's gone to weep in the stairwell.

"No, I am saying I'll ask her about her wishes. If she isn't coherent enough to know, we should proceed with the surgery."

Dianna trudges back into the hospital room. Dr. Kumar has no idea how disturbed her mother is. Mary Ann comes in carrying a wad of tissues and slumps into a corner chair. Dianna steels herself as she always does before any encounter with her mother. She doesn't want Mama to die—she is, after all, her mother. All she can do is make a decision based on what she *thinks* her mother would want. It seems she doesn't stand much chance either way, and the surgery seems to be her mother's only hope.

"Dianna, I asked you to clean me up," her mother slurs. "Where were you?"

"Talking to your doctor, Mama." Dianna walks over and puts her hands on the bed rails.

"That German? You shouldn't be talking to Germans."

Dianna suppresses an irritated laugh. "Mama, World War II has been over for almost five decades. The cardiologist, who is *American,* says you need surgery, but it is dangerous surgery." She reaches out and pats her mother's wrist.

"I don't want a German operating on me."

"It's the only chance you've got, Mama," she says with a stern tone she does not feel. She hopes her mother can't read her expression like she used to. She moves around the room, straightening, wetting a washcloth, and searching for a bed pan.

Her mother begins to shake. "I should have done it when I had the chance," she wails. "I should have taken all those pills when you were little, before the other two came along. I was a good person then."

"What do you want now, Mama?" Dianna pretends she hasn't heard her, moving closer to get her mother's attention. She hadn't wanted to lose her mother, even on the day of the pills, though she resigned herself to the fact she probably would. She had been so young then, so scared. She doesn't feel any less frightened today.

Why must she be responsible for everyone?

"I want to go home," her mother whispers, and the river of tears slows. Her mother grabs her hand, just as she did when Dianna was a teenager. Her nails dig into Dianna's palm. "Those people when I was asleep," she looks at Dianna straight in the eye, "they told me I was mean. They told me I should apologize."

Dianna pats her mother's hand with her free one, adjusts the wires, and fluffs the pillows. "It's okay, Mama. I know you're sorry. I know you couldn't help it."

"I want to go home," her mother says again. "Dianna, take me home."

Dr. Kumar stands in silhouette in the doorway. He comes in with soft, velvet steps and presses the call button, beckoning for the women to follow him once more.

"You'll die if I take you home, Mama."

"Not that home. I mean, I want my real home!"

Dianna squeezes her mother's hand and then walks out of the room.

Her mother begins wailing. "I want to be well! I want to be well! Take me home or let me die!"

Where is home, exactly?

Dianna's breath comes out in short clips when they reach the incandescent hallway. "I can't know what she wants," she tells Mary Ann and the doctor.

"I usually tell children to put themselves in their parents' shoes," the doctor replies and touches her arm again.

When did her mother ever want what her daughter did? Yet, her own viewpoint is all she's got to go on.

Her words come out clipped and sharp. "She's having the surgery," she tells the doctor. "Let's set her free, one way or the other."

• • •

Mary Ann, T.C., and Dianna are driving to the neighborhood cafeteria. They have been waiting since dawn for some word on the outcome of the surgery, and T.C. can wait no longer. T.C. and hospitals don't mix, plus he's always hungry, so they get into Mary Ann's Chrysler and head out.

They pass a mile or so of highway construction. "The government sold this land to developers," Mary Ann comments.

The construction crew has already begun tearing down a swathe of fir trees to widen the road and begin a driveway into what will be a new high-priced development wedged into a small space. Farmland around the hospital is now prime building land, and this is one of the last available parcels.

They stop at a light, and Mary Ann pats her foot up and down on the accelerator to ensure they don't stall. Could all these buildings have been woodland only a few years ago? She turns around to ask T.C., but he's blocked out the world with his Walkman. T.C.'s been like this his whole life. If the going gets rough, he checks out. He's made sure life doesn't pass him too many surprises, taking night classes, working days at the local landscaping nursery, a job he's now lost. Hunting, fishing, never staying still at family gatherings. Present but absent.

Dianna decides not to push him. It's a difficult day for them all. She turns back around in the front passenger seat, and her eyes catch sight of something, a golden red sheen shining in the sun. It's a fox, stranded on the median beside them. The fox's eyes tilt to one side, and she runs that way, only to be met by a row of cars. So, she course-corrects the other way, only to meet another wall of cars. Dianna focuses on her beautiful golden eyes, wild with terror and frustration. They dart in one direction, meet an obstacle, dart in another, meet another obstruction. Why doesn't she just lie down and wait until nightfall?

Animals don't quit. They keep trying until the end, no matter how panicked they become. She's heard stories about animals biting off their paws to escape traps.

Then she sees the kits mewing on the other side of the highway. One tries to jump down but rolls back.

"That fox is going to get run over." She turns and taps T.C. on the knee. "T.C., can't we do something to save it?"

With a look of annoyance, T.C. turns off his music and takes off his earphones. "What?"

"That fox. Isn't there anything we can do?"

"I don't have my gun. Call the SPCA," T.C. says, his tone off-putting, and he puts the earphones back on. Dianna taps his knee again, and T.C. jerks the earphones back down. "What, Dianna?! What now?"

"Come on, T.C. Have a heart," Mary Ann calls into the back seat.

"He's just a wild animal." T.C. sneers. "If a car doesn't get him, a bullet will. If not a bullet, then the first snow."

Dianna turns back around in her seat, defeated. "Is that what it's all about, then? If one thing doesn't get you, another will?"

Mary Ann pats her arm. "Dianna, the fox has been in the wild a long time. He can take care of himself."

Dianna lets out a muffled groan. "It's female."

They enter the cafeteria parking lot and walk to the long line for fried okra and ham biscuits. T.C. piles his plate high. Even Mary Ann takes her share.

"I'm not hungry," Dianna says. "Just tea for me, thanks." She's still with the mother fox. Then with her dying mother, her dead father, Qasim, Khalil, herself. All that love. Wasted. To Death. She excuses herself and goes to the restroom to shed a few tears. She flushes the toilet, a left-over habit from her bulimic days. Sheds a few more tears. Washes her face off. Searches for a non-existent paper towel. Only air dryers. Such is progress. Such is life. She unrolls the toilet paper to blow her nose.

She returns to her siblings, who eat in perfect, absolute silence. T.C. still has his earphones on. Mary Ann is lost in thought. Dianna bites her nails.

Mary Ann returns to the hospital via a different route, she says to avoid the heavy traffic. The traffic doesn't seem any lighter. Dr. Kumar awaits them in the front corridor, still in his scrubs. "I'm sorry," he says, simply and sadly. "I'm sorry." And then those clichéd words: "We did everything we could." His eyes fill up with tears, which betray the cliché. This is the first person she's liked since she returned. Maybe there *is* hope.

Her siblings stand looking at him for a while, then hug each other, hugging Dianna last. They sit. They stare. The seconds tick past until a nurse arrives with a strained look.

"Which funeral home?" she asks without introduction.

The three of them turn their stares on her.

"Where do you want her sent?" the nurse asks. "We have to get her out of here."

CHAPTER TWELVE:
OZYMANDIAS

July 5, 1991
Richfield, North Carolina

It's one day in a string of days full of mourning. A day before the probate estate matters take over her life. A day after the neighbors stopped bringing casseroles.

Dianna's sitting on her mother's bed. The afternoon light swirls around the dust clouds she's stirring up, sorting through her mother's belongings.

T.C. stands half in, half out of the room, ready to bolt through the open door should she pull out something unsavory. The sunlight catches and glints off a "for sale" through the windowpane. It's nearing dusk, and there's much more to be done.

When she looks up, tears sweep down T.C.'s cheeks, the first she's seen from him since childhood. "You okay?"

He just nods.

She pulls out a wool blue hand-knit sweater, a pair of reading glasses missing one lens, a five-year-old Reader's Digest, a church bulletin from the Sunday before her mother was hospitalized, a piece of a broken teacup, and a string of mustard-colored beads.

"Mind if I take those?" T.C. crosses the room like a gust of wind and pulls their late mother's belongings to his chest.

"No, of course not," Dianna says, but she clings to the sweater. She'd like to have it wrapped around her, like a pair of nurturing arms. A mother she had for only an instant, if at all.

T.C. weeps into the pile of wood and plastic. "I can't believe she's gone. Why did you let her die?"

"I did think she'd live forever. She had a will to live like the Energizer Bunny." She hands him a box of Kleenex. "Here. Take this, too." She won't answer to T.C.'s grief. He has to have someone to blame.

She needs to get back to business. Here's a bright floral rayon dress with a zipper down the front. She's ready to hold it up in front of the mirror. She needs clothes. But here comes Mary Ann down the hall. She nestles in her grandmother's old rocker, wrapping another of her mother's pilled sweaters around her as though it's cold on this warm day. "She certainly did dress loud at the end."

They all break into giggles, and Dianna throws the dress in the giveaway box. "Mary Ann, want anything out of this box?"

"No, it's mostly trash now anyway, isn't it?" Mary Ann rolls her eyes, making certain their brother doesn't see. "T.C., can you come check on my car?" She winks at Dianna. "I can't get it to start."

T.C. wipes his hand across his cheeks, ignoring the Kleenex.

"Alright." He takes his pile of mementos along with him. T.C. is a basket case. She can't leave him alone. She'll have to return to New York and look for another job.

Dianna's reaching the bottom of the box. She pulls out a comb with a few teeth left, a crushed lipstick tube, and a hot water bottle. Then she pulls out what she's been saving for last—the family Bible her mother took with her everywhere. Not much different than any other leather-bound edition, yet it contains their family genealogy. Written in precise script, her great grandmother began it, and her mother finished it with T.C. Dianna rubs a finger over the name: Thomas Caldwell Calloway in her mother's cursive, the year of birth in carefully scripted numerals. Who would write in his date of death? None of them have children.

She wants the pages to come to life, to tell the stories her family tree's branches hold. But all she sees is writing, and all she hears is Mary Ann's motor turning over. They'll return in a moment. She flips through the Biblical passages, some underlined, the notes in the margins in seven different hands, and takes out slips of paper, envelopes holding baby curls, and photos along the way.

A photo catches her eye. It's of her mother and a man holding hands. Her mother must have been about eighteen. She's laughing, vibrant, as though the man just told a good joke. She turns the photo over: "To Louisa Anna. My Love Forever." It was signed Willard, 1940. Long before her father. She's never heard of such a man.

A letter she's missed falls out to the floor. It's a letter from her mother to her high school friend. No envelope or stamp. Was it ever mailed?

My Dear Mimi,

How long has it been? How I wish I could be with you. Where are you now? I read your letters, and then I forget I've read them. I go in and out of this fog. Sometimes it seems you are here, sitting next to me. I don't think the women here are mailing my letters.

My children are all grown. Mary Ann is the only one who comes to see me. I don't know what's become of T.C., but that may be my mind. Dianna is in Africa. She sends me pictures sometimes. I wish I could change some things between us, but you know, I'm human. People make mistakes, tears in the seam of life.

What we remain is mother and son, mother and daughter. Dianna's made her way in the world, despite my problems. That's what I've wanted for all my children. I wish I could have done what I wished for. I was so disappointed. I'm glad she's used her gifts. After all, as you remember, I named her Dianna for a reason.

Love Always,

Louisa Anna

As T.C. bursts into the room, Dianna stuffs the undated letter, the photo, and all the other documents in her pocket. "Finished?" he asks, glancing at the empty box. "Find anything else?"

"Just the Bible."

"Can I . . ."

"You can have it." Dianna shoves it into his arms and escapes the room.

Chapter Thirteen: Hostage Release

December 1, 1991
New York City

New York seems the obvious place to begin looking for a job. It's where her career began. She's still patching up the pieces of her mother's withered life like a puzzle salvaged from a flooded basement. Her life also needs some mending. Her life has been one step by uneven step at a time. Now she can think of the future in more than one-day increments. Now she can find old friends who used to support her. They will again.

She's brought the last of her mother's belongings to go through here, away from T.C. She tosses a moth-eaten sweater and afghan that have seen better days. She keeps the sentimental: her great grandmother's brooch, the ring her father gave her mother for their fifth anniversary, a tiny, varnished silver jewelry box, its top unhinged. She's U-Hauled a few tattered pieces of furniture from the shed out back and picked up some odds and ends at the flea market to accentuate them. Period pieces. 1950s Modern. Not her style, but good enough for now. T.C. had wanted most everything, and he was brewing for an argument. She and Mary Ann had split the jewelry. Mary Ann kept the good furniture, her mother's other rings nestled in her good jewelry box, and all her mother's reading glasses.

Sad to think this is all that remains of her parents' time here on Earth. She hopes to leave more behind, not a material legacy but a tug at certain people's hearts. So far, she doubts she has.

Her own heart beats in fits and starts. Some days, tears sting at her eyes, so much so she's bought a pair of sunglasses for the first time. Other days, her heart seems not to beat at all.

Memories zing her at inopportune moments, but she has to keep going. She's dipped into her retirement. She must pay the bills. All the while trying to support two siblings who seem lost with or without her. Maybe a better sister would've stayed and cared for them. Could she have made a difference?

On days when she can sort through no more grief, she calls on long-ago friends and colleagues, searching for job leads: Leah, her old roomie, Sophia, a refugee from Hungarian royalty, and Heather, who's finally turned her twenty-something drama around and become a high-ranking Wall Street economist.

Today, Dianna weaves in between parked cars on her way to the Met to have lunch with Sophia, who'd been both boss and fairy godmother to her. They're starting to computerize at the museum. She walks up the familiar steps, through the three-domed entrance, where she sat most workdays and some weekends looking at the newspaper, the photos coming to life and giving her strength to leave the museum and follow her dreams.

The colored button badges are still at the entrance, although they've added new pastel hues to the primary colors. She even thinks she may recognize a couple of the guards, but they have stopped opening doors for visitors. Most look too young to have been there when she was, and she sees one chewing gum. It would have been forbidden in the early 1980s.

She hesitates in the museum's entranceway, and in memory, she can almost see Qasim's green four-door sedan weave in and out of a thread of Checker cabs and pull up short at the curb. She can see the wave of Qasim's hand, the rising moon glinting on his long fingers, and the muted plaid of his suit jacket. Where were they going that day? If she'd remained, what would have happened? Had he been trying to come back to her in Africa?

• • •

Sophia is still beautiful, the angles of her face pronounced, her body lithe, her smile warm.

"Dianna, dear," Sophia says in her elegant voice, part honey, part chestnut. She gives her a hug for the ages. A perfect New York hug. Dianna feels safe in her company even after all this time apart. Just like before, when security was a priceless commodity for her. If only she were seeing her again after her success in South Africa instead of her failure in Sudan. She's told Sophia about her mother's recent death, but she doesn't want Sophia's pity, only her friendship.

"Come." Sophia motions to her. "Let me show you the new exhibits. You cataloged some of these pieces when you were here."

The exhibits have been shuffled, changed, retouched, or stored. A new European Sculpture courtyard with skylights and statuary graces the Central Park wing, but the brickwork of the original 1880s exterior wall remains. She used to jog past the beautiful brickwork when it was exposed to the elements. The staircases from the Chicago Exchange Building have been moved to this section. They lead only to a balcony now, not offices with voices, shouted bidding, the ringing of the starting bell.

They drift on to her favorite pieces, still in their proper places: the Roman sarcophagus, the museum's first acquisition, the Frank Lloyd Wright windows, and the eight-thousand-year-old stone figure from Syria or Mesopotamia. The archaeologists still haven't identified its original home. To Dianna, it looks more like a mother and child every time she encounters it, the gracious female curves and the crossed arms still quite visible, nestling what must have once been an infant. And, of course, the Faience vessel. Its vivid colors still fascinate her: blue turquoise, yellow-brown, flowers that look like edelweiss on top of bowls of fruit, fish, dragons, and bulls in battle. Layers of history in one small container. A dead fly lies near the vessel, like a present-day offering to this long-ago era.

They head to the café, and Sophia takes the check before Dianna can protest. Then they head outside to enjoy this surprising autumnal weather, taking their tea with them. "I'm elated you're visiting," Sophia says.

The number of chestnut and pretzel vendors has grown sparse, and so has the smoke that drifted through the air from their wares. The subway fare has risen forty cents, and the cars seem cleaner and less threatening. She's heard the old immigration buildings on Ellis Island reopened as a museum last year. This year, the last automat closed. "Lost in Yonkers" and "Angels in America" are the hottest things on Broadway, which seems dingier than ever. Homeless people, ill with the HIV/AIDS virus, unknown about a decade ago, wander the streets in increasing numbers. She's seen her share of people with AIDS in Africa, but she didn't know how it had ravaged her home. Disease doesn't discriminate between the developed and developing world.

"What happened to Map Man?" she asks Sophia. Map Man was homeless and sat on the steps poring over maps. He always looked like he was searching for a lost land. Her first lesson about boundaries and borders, he taught her. Despite her cushy job at a New York Museum, he'd inspired her to keep going for her dream, to help the world.

"He just disappeared," Sophia says. "I suppose he must have died."

She walks and sifts through memories of AIDS, then of famine, then of Khalil. She would wither and die if she found he's contracted AIDS. A funny thing, memory. Razor sharp with things you'd rather forget. Fuzzy like cotton candy when you want to retain it.

"So, how is life at the Met?" Dianna asks, a bit rueful, a bit sarcastic.

"Same as always. *Plus ça change*. Here, Dianna, have some of my tea."

"Right, New York is more New York than ever." Dianna looks down at her now-empty cup. "I was thinking of my mother and I having tea yesterday." She doesn't let Sophia know her mind is with her mother most of the time, the mother she knew in childhood. She might as well be in North Carolina instead of here.

"I'm sorry you've lost her so early. You must miss her."

"I miss the earlier days. I've missed them for years, though."

"Did she bring out the silver service at your tea?" Sophia's smile is wry. She knows about Dianna's Southern background.

"It was more picnic. We sat in my grandmother's field. We visited her every summer. The grass was tall enough to encircle us in a cocoon. My mother spread the red gingham tablecloth down, smoothing the grass underneath, and we sat close, two rabbits in their burrow."

"I can see the two of you."

"She'd just given me a new blue willow tea set for my birthday. We set it up for high tea. And the tea was real with made-from-scratch sugar cookies, hand-picked wild blackberries, and thick cream for the strong tea she poured into our tiny little girl cups. We slurped the tea up and told our own made-up fairy tales."

Hers had been a tale about a bunny that lost its cottontail. Her mother had told a story about ballerinas riding horses. Before the illness fell upon her, she had loved storytelling.

"How are you, Dianna?" Sophia is asking.

She hopes she hasn't seen her moist eyes. "I'm doing fine. Just memories flooding in. I'm surprised. After all the time she was sick, her death took me off guard."

"So, you're looking for a job," Sophia says more than asks.

"Yes, I've got to pay the rent. The traveling life is over for a while. My brother and sister still need my help, too. I'm surprised how much I miss my mother, after all we'd been through, how long she'd been ill."

"Sudan must have been horrible."

"It was worse than the other countries . . . Kenya, Tanzania, South Africa, Zimbabwe. The people welcomed me in Nairobi, Natal, and Addis. Sudan made me stronger. And wiser." Dianna searches for a smile but cannot find it. "Seeing the children die is the worst."

"Dianna," Sophia picks up her spoon, twirls it in her tapered fingers, and puts it down again. "Do you think you could go back to typing little green cards here after Sudan?"

Dianna shakes her head. She knew the answer to this question before she sat down with Sophia.

"That's what awaits you here at the Met," Sophia says. "That's what my middle-aged life has entailed. I'm just hanging on for retirement." She says this with no hint of resentment or regret.

"I don't know where else to go," Dianna says, trying to keep the remorse and desperation out of her voice.

"Isn't Operation Ready to Read connected to the U.N.? You could look there for a stateside job. I also have a friend at the U.N. I could put you in touch with her." Sophia ticks off her list on her fingers. "Plus . . ."

"I don't know, Sophia. I left Sudan under some heavy scrutiny." Dianna feels her face redden.

"Come on, Dianna. They'll have already forgotten. I can't imagine what infraction such a competent, compassionate, experienced U.N. worker could have made that would cause them never to talk to you again. How big is the United Nations? How can they possibly let one minor problem destroy your otherwise stellar record?" She pauses. "You did have an otherwise stellar record, right? I know you."

Dianna nods, perhaps with too much enthusiasm. She doesn't

want to tell Sophia that she almost went rogue. She's amazed at her actions then. Time can yield perspective, but it can also yield ignorance and indifference. Even if they don't care as much about her actions, they may have forgotten she exists.

"Well, then, it's settled." Sophia looks ready to suggest something else but then clamps her mouth shut as though she's thought better of it. "How's your love life, Dianna?"

Dianna feels her face pinken. Unlike her, Sophia has a string of lovers like some women have a string of pearls, all devoted to her until she dumps them.

All the casual, blind dates Dianna's been on lately, trying to forget the last few years, aren't the answer. The guy with the grunt that was supposed to be a laugh. The man who came to dinner unshowered in his jogging outfit. Another who seemed to be right, with an Irish brogue just like the boy she abandoned for Africa long ago, but who had two other girlfriends. None of them are Qasim.

"I mainly meet divorced men who cancel dates at the last minute to spend a few precious moments with a son or daughter." A son like Qasim had. She should have comprehended then why he needed to wait to introduce her.

Sophia's mouth turns down in disappointment. How could a beautiful woman like her understand Dianna's dilemma?

"There was the guy that jumped me and bit my tongue." She's already laughing. "Unmarried."

"What!"

"Yes, he brought me flowers, took me to the Village for music and drinks, and then bit my tongue because I wouldn't go home with him."

"How horrible!" Sophia's eyes widen with something like shock.

"Pretty normal these days. I've just about given up on men."

"I do understand that, my dear," Sophia says. "After all, I haven't found 'him' either. Though I continue to try."

"Oh, Sophia, you always had suitors lined up, waiting for your daughter to grow up. I never had that. At all."

"Not true. You just didn't look around, Dianna."

"Shall we go?" Dianna wants to end this conversation. She doesn't want to talk about Qasim. "This has been lovely. Thank you."

"No, thank *you*," Sophia says and hugs her. She pauses, and this time the words come. "Dianna, isn't there anyone else at the U.N. you'd like to call? You would be a proficient translator, but with your fieldwork, you could do so much more if you had an 'in.'"

"No." Dianna tries to keep her tone soft, but it ends up abrupt. "I'll find my way there. I always have."

"I'm here if you need me. You've lost both your parents. I still have my mother, and I'm twenty years older than you." Sophia is looking at her with a puzzled expression. She probably does not feel she knows Dianna any longer.

Dianna pulls the letter from her mother out of her pocketbook. "Let's go sit on the bench. I have something to read to you," she tells Sophia. She pulls her by the hand as a child would, but Sophia follows without protest.

Dianna reads the letter and then gives it to Sophia, who re-reads passages. "I wish I could say these things about my daughter."

"This was the only time she ever did say them," Dianna says, and a sob cracks through.

"Oh, sweetie," Sophia whispers, tears in her eyes, a huskiness to her normally velvet voice. She hugs Dianna like a sister would—no, like a mother would. She hasn't cried like this since she was eleven. She registers the people who pass and stare at them, but only with a vague sense of relinquishing their judgment.

She's lost in this embrace, in this moment, in this grief that has bided its time for acknowledgment. Then she stops, no tears left.

"Sweetie, this may not be the time for me to pursue this question, but . . ." Sophia licks her lips as if searching for the right word.

"Go ahead. I can hear anything now." Dianna smiles.

"Didn't Qasim work for the U.N.? Have you thought about where he is?" Sophia plays with a lock of Dianna's long hair.

"Oh, Sophia, how I miss him!"

Chapter Fourteen: Missing in Action

January 23, 1992
New York City

Dianna doesn't know what she'll do or say when she sees Qasim, but a feeling is surfacing, compelling her to find him, like a whale responding to another whale's underwater clicks. A bird who somehow knows her migration route from the first year until the very last year of her life. Imprints . . . isn't that what they call them? His voice is somehow imprinted on her, and she can hear him calling.

She dials the number he gave her. It's disconnected. She tries once a day for three days, always with the same result.

She sheds tears for a time. Does he carry cards in his pockets with numbers that no longer work? Did he give her an old card because he no longer wanted to hear from her? The younger Dianna would have given up at this point, concocted reasons he was eluding her, and wallowed in thoughts of abandonment, distrust, and lack of love. This time, she wants to know the truth.

She goes to the U.N. for an interview in the translations department and mentions his name to a few people. No one has heard of him. Then she stands in the lobby as though he could appear at her whim. Appear as he did in the embassy, as if he had known she was there. Her investigation is a mixture of method and madness. Deep inside, she knows he is not in the States. He told her he was going to the Middle East, then back to Africa.

Finally, she ventures up to the reception desk. "Hello, I'm Dianna Calloway," she says, trying to seem nonchalant, as though she has a right to inquire about his whereabouts.

The woman behind the desk has a blunt haircut and a scowl. Dianna readies herself for a struggle.

"I have an appointment with Qasim el-Kafry."

The woman looks down at Dianna and smiles. "Identification, please," she says with the slightest West African intonation. She wears a dark blue standard-issue U.N. uniform with African earrings that remind Dianna of zebra hide.

The woman gazes at Dianna's driver's license, then back up to her face. She smiles. "What time is your appointment?"

She has misjudged this woman. This won't be as much of a negotiation as she thought. She glances at her watch. It is 10:45. "Eleven o'clock," She smiles back.

The receptionist clicks her computer mouse over and over. Dianna begins to perspire. "How do you spell his last name, Miss?"

Dianna spells the name twice. Then she spells his first name. She feels the thud of her heart with every letter.

The woman frowns in concentration and keeps clicking. "Which department did you say?"

Dianna's heart sinks into her gut. If he were here, the receptionist would have found him in the database by now.

"I'm uncertain." Her heart begins to race. She digs into her pocket and pulls out his card.

The woman continues her computer search, then pulls out a paper directory. "I can find no Qasim el-Kafry here, Miss. Perhaps he is at one of the NGOs?"

Dianna thanks her for her time, shrugs into her coat, and walks back into the rain. She stands, staring, seeing him in her mind, walking away through the airport crowds. Will she ever see him again?

This is melodramatic poetry at best and fantasy at worst. Nevertheless, once home, she combs the telephone book. He's not there.

How could this relationship possibly work, especially over oceans and continents? Sitting on her frayed couch, she opens and closes the box he gave her, which she had repaired. He is an Arab, divorce or no divorce, whose life is built on ambition, image, and, yes, fear. She knows now she heard fear in his voice when he told her not to come care for him when he was so ill before their break-up in 1983, not fear of her but of himself. And she listened to that voice because she had been afraid, too. He was afraid of her seeing him hurt, and she was afraid of hurting the both of them.

Monday, she calls a former colleague in Egypt and asks her to look in the Cairo and Beirut phone books. Nothing.

Wednesday, she calls the public relations office at the U.N. and asks if they have any press releases about him, with no result.

Thursday, she calls the contact Sophia gave her. Not a trace.

Short of putting out an APB, she has exhausted her resources.

The translations department calls her in the afternoon for a second interview. The next week, they offer her the job. They also offer to pay for further schooling. Her days are full of words, and her evenings are full of books. Yet a piece of her travels with him in her night dreams.

CHAPTER FIFTEEN:
LOST AND FOUND

October 22, 1992
New York City

Dianna is reading an Arabic language textbook and stir-frying vegetables. She glances over at the kitchen table, which, instead of being set for dinner, is full of documents that need to be translated for tomorrow. Kofi Annan is in town, which always means more work for her. Everyone defers to him. Rumor has it he'll soon be named Undersecretary General. She's getting too old for all-nighters. She needs to get out for her run before the night air turns chilly.

She's settled into a routine she's unsure she enjoys. Busy, yes. Fulfilled, not so much. The oil pops up onto her finger, and she jumps. "Ouch!" She rummages around in the cabinet above the stove for some baking soda, her family's chief remedy for burns, passed down instead of china or unconditional love.

When her downstairs buzzer goes off, Dianna is still picking through spices and jelly jars. Resentment rises in her throat. Who could it be? Everyone knows how busy she is these days.

She buzzes the person in without even asking for identification and returns to her baking soda search. She hears the key grind in the lock at her front door. It's Leah. Her former apartment mate lives downstairs; she helped Dianna find this apartment last year. They sort of share apartments, coming and going at will from one abode to the other.

"Sorry to bother you." Leah grimaces. "Did I leave my key here last night? I can't find it anywhere. I'll get out as soon as I find it."

Dianna sticks her burned finger in her mouth, resigned to not finding the baking soda. She dishes her vegetables on a plate and puts a few on another for Leah. "Look around. It's probably here." Leah is always losing something.

Dianna left for her first African assignment when Leah worked for the mayor, but they've stayed close through letters. Leah was her lifeline when she was on a tough assignment. She'd wept about disease and death to Leah on paper, and Leah didn't tell her to stop writing. It was nice to know a friend in the U.S. who understood what was happening in African countries.

"Sorry," Leah says again.

"I just don't have much time tonight, okay? But stay and eat." Dianna hears the anxiety in her words, even as she begins to clear the table and Leah fishes out silverware. "I guess I have a few minutes to chat while I eat."

Leah searches all the usual hiding spots: the rickety coffee table, the faded olive-green sofa cushions, the tile floor, the mossy faux Oriental carpet. She sighs and comes to the table. "Maybe it's in my apartment. I didn't have it when I left last night, though."

"You'll find it." Dianna pats her hand. "Come on, Leah; stay and eat. How was your day?"

Leah's shock of red hair hides her expression. She's good at seeming fine when she's not, her face always inscrutable, her hands always steady, and her New York fashion sense covering any lack of composure. Her old toughness has smoothed out a little, but she's still not one to share much vulnerability. Leah can put an outfit together from nothing, the way some people can make a three-course dinner out of eggs. Yet she can never find the essentials, like keys.

"You look great tonight," Dianna says.

"Thanks."

Dianna starts to pick at her stir fry, then gulps the vegetables down, surprising herself at her hunger. "What's up, Leah?" She can tell Leah came up for more than keys.

"Cameron, that jerk."

"Oh no." Cameron had seemed so attentive, said all the right words. "It seemed to be going so well. Why do men have to be so off and on?"

"That's life in the big city, I guess." Leah sniffs. "Maybe I will have a little stir fry after all. It smells delish." She takes a bite. "Do you think we'll ever be eating dinner with a man across the table from us?" She looks around the room with a wistful smirk, then rallies. "Dianna, what's with this card table after all these years? You're a grown-up. Go get a real wooden dining table. Some matching chairs."

Dianna winces. Leah had a designer furnish her own apartment last year. Dianna's apartment blends the old and the new. Plus, this place is the first she could call her own. "I don't think about it much. The man or the furniture. Maybe I'm just a nomad. Something is missing. I just don't know how to find it. It's like your lost key. You think you know where you left it, but you just don't know where to look."

"Unrequited love," Leah says in a *sotto voce*, giving her a wise but sarcastic smile that means they both know she's right, but Dianna won't own up to it.

"There's got to be some nice guy out there for us."

Leah had been attracted to Qasim a decade ago, but not for love. She'd wanted to use his connections, so she'd wedged doubt in Dianna's mind about whether the relationship could work.

"That was the whole problem in the 80s," Leah says, and Dianna gives her a look warning her not to continue. The past is the past. "They're all three-legged jerks," Leah says, and they have a good laugh. "Good stir fry." Leah gets up and gives Dianna a big hug. "Thanks."

"I apologize. I was so short with you. There'll be other men. There always are, one way or the other."

"No, no. Sorry I bothered you on such a busy night," Leah says. "I know how you are, always working. No pangs of guilt allowed, okay? Just study, or translate, or finish eating. One more pass-through, and I'll be on my way."

Her hand runs underneath the frayed sofa cushions one last time. Then she opens the box of her mother's sentimental belongings. Dianna is about to warn her that her keys can't be in there.

"What's this?" Leah pulls out a book that looks like a journal, with papers stuffed inside. The papers fly everywhere.

"Oh, it's my mother's old papers. I need to go through them."

Leah gasps. On the floor are six newspaper clippings and some letters in Qasim's hand.

They both fall to the floor and pick them up. The first is an article from Lebanon's daily English newspaper. "New research. Hope you are well," he's jotted on the side column. He'd given Dianna an article when they were together on similar research. She'd read it to her mother over the phone, wondering if her mother's already fading memory could comprehend it. It turns out she had because that article isn't here, but two others are.

Three other articles about experimental health research are there, too, a tiny third column next to all the war coverage. One says, "I hope Dianna is well. Please give her my warmest regards."

"I need a moment," Dianna says. She moves to the sofa and presses her fist into her belly to ease the ache, the shock.

"Listen to the last one," Leah says. "It's a photo of Qasim and a bunch of men at what they say is Beirut's Parliament Building ages ago. 'Dr. Qasim el-Kafry, the front runner for Parliament, stands with The Hon. Dr. Jamal el-Baydun. Dr. el-Kafry's reformist platform emphasizes social justice, a transparent economy, and a recalibrated, rotating party system, which would include a new Census.' It says he wants to carve out a workable government and end the civil war. *That* didn't happen."

"He looks so handsome," Dianna says after she's stared at it for a long time. "I guess Jamal did get him on the ticket, but he must have lost. I despise Jamal."

"So, you're not angry with me? I didn't help matters." She looks as though she's afraid. Dianna must look like she's holding a grenade instead of a letter. That's the way the weight of the letter feels in her hand.

"No, nothing you could've done would've made any difference in him returning home. Not with Jamal coercing him into going back. He loved his country more than any person."

"Why do you think he sent these articles to your mother?" Leah asks, her eyes wide.

The pieces of her past float by in her mind. She's attempting to put the puzzle together. She's angry and confused he wrote her mother and not her. He never answered her last letter. "I don't know. He cared about people who suffered."

"No." Leah's voice is piercing. "He loved you, Dianna. Don't ever doubt it." She hands Dianna the rest of the papers and letters.

"I'm not sure I can finish reading these letters." Dianna wants to run from the apartment, run until she passes out, to stop the pain of the past as it surges in.

"You must. I'll sit beside you," Leah whispers, grasping Diana's hand. "I never knew this was so deep."

"What?" Then Diana begins to read the letters, too. Her mother and Qasim had been correspondents. The letters are personal and detailed. Qasim talks about his family, the never-ending war—and how much he misses Dianna. He acknowledges how much her mother misses her, too.

Dianna feels something jagged tear open in her chest, but the pain lessens the more she reads. She'd assumed he'd sat in Parliament for a few terms, but he didn't even make it into Parliament. She's heartbroken for him. For Lebanon. She's heartbroken for herself, for what could have been.

The last letter is dated five years ago, around the time her mother lost almost all her mental faculties. He probably stopped writing because she didn't—couldn't—respond. He must have suspected. He probably knew this was his last letter to her. And he was afraid to tell Dianna he'd been trying to keep up with her.

"Please let Dianna know how much she meant to me," he writes. "I am so proud of her career in Africa. I always saw it in her. I wish we could have done it together, but I'm beyond admiration she's doing it solo. If any woman—*anyone*—can make a difference, it is your daughter Dianna."

Dianna shoves the letters back into Leah's hands. She rushes to the bathroom, locks the door, and turns on the faucet. For a long time, she looks into the gilt mirror above the sink, an artifact from her childhood. The last time she locked herself in a bathroom, she did it for secrecy. This time, she wants only privacy. She no longer needs to lift the toilet lid to rid herself of all that nurtured her body. She's learned to feel.

When she finally opens the door, Leah has cleaned up the dishes and stowed the letters back in the box.

"Found my keys!"

"Where were they?"

"They'd dropped under the dining room table. They were there all along."

"Like Qasim."

Leah smiles. She looks exhausted. Dianna feels the same way. "Thanks for cleaning."

"Of course, Dianna. Are you okay? Will you be okay?"

"Leah, I'm always okay. I think once I wrap my mind around this new information, it will help me heal, have closure."

"Oh, this isn't closure from the sound of it." Leah's smile broadens. She strolls out the door, all elegance and charm and New York sophisticated.

Qasim had cared for her enough to hold a door open until she was ready to care for herself. She loves him now more than ever. She tries to wash off her tears at the sink, but they keep flowing. She's unable to tell where the stream of water washing down the drain begins and where her tears begin any more than she can determine where he ends and she begins.

Where would she be without him?

No running tonight. Dianna returns to fishing the meaning out of other people's words, but her eyes are heavy. She may not meet her deadline.

CHAPTER SIXTEEN:
PERSONA NON GRATA

November 23, 1992
United Nations Building
Manhattan

Dianna sits on the edge of her chair, legs uncrossed, feet on the floor, hands resting in her lap. They've placed her in the middle of a small circle of interviewers. They might as well be called interrogators. Their faces are soft with compassion, but their questions are sharp.

She's increased her applications in the past few months, and she's received several calls to interview. International humanitarian interviews are like none other. They involve layers, at least three. The first is with three or four people, professionals but not senior staff. If you pass muster, the interview involves numerous managers, a staff psychologist, at least one head of department, and usually a peace worker from the field. The circle becomes small again for the final interview. The panel dissolves into two or three superiors, one of whom you'll be working for. Human resources is almost always represented. If only they'd staff the field as well as they did the Secretariat!

Dianna is good at interviews. She had to pretend for her parents for a childhood, so she can shift and maneuver, and she's good at wearing a costume that doesn't exactly fit her but comes off as if it does. She could've been an actor if she'd had more self-confidence in her body. She's got that confidence now.

"Describe how you've participated in a successful teamwork experience," demands the human resources director.

Dianna almost knows this answer by rote. She works well in teams or alone. She talks about the team she led in Nairobi. She ends with a plea. "I'd prefer to be placed in a team in the field," she says. "I like knowing the decisions are not mine alone and that someone has my back just like I have theirs. But I'm fine on my own, truly. I demonstrated that in a couple of missions already."

She's already been through a written test, a language fluency oral and written examination. She passed her competency-based interview. This is the first time she's been short-listed since Sudan. Plus, this position is in Ethiopia, her part of the world, and she tells them so. This is more a development job than a relief or teaching position. Only one thing leaves her uncertain, and that is talking about her work history—her time in Southern Sudan.

The man she believes to be her future manager raises an eyebrow but remains silent.

"I understand that decisions in the field are paradoxical and often unfair," she says, and she makes herself relax into her chair as his eyebrow descends. Maybe she can convince him, after all of her worth, that she is not a rule breaker or, worse, a fanatic.

"Describe a situation when you had to be creative," says the peacekeeper. He seems to want to move away from any kind of confrontation. He mediates peace for a living, after all.

Dianna settles into this question. She's in her element when she must employ creative decision-making. She looks each interviewer in the eyes.

"I'm an out-of-the-box thinker."

"I got a water team into a village when all roads were barricaded. I first sent a colleague I managed to negotiate with the military."

"When a particular negotiation or mediation didn't work, I (and my team) tried another route and another. There's always a win-win solution . . . eventually." She wonders if she believes this last statement.

Everyone nods in approval except for her probable future boss. She talks about another project where she solved a big problem.

"Tell us about your experience with seeing life from an African perspective," interjects the head of mission before she can say more. They must have approved of her last two answers.

"I've worked nowhere except Africa," she says, and her spine straightens in pride. She tells them a few aid-worker stories, careful to make herself look like the hero at times but also to show what she's learned from her few mistakes. Skirting clear of Southern Sudan. "I love the African people," she concludes. "I would do almost anything for them, and I find it best to lend them my advice but let them make the final decisions. People talk about corruption, but on the ground, it's rare."

Uh-oh, she may have said the wrong thing there. She's almost pointed them in the direction of her relationship with Biel.

She inhales because she knows the question about her past will come from her direct report. She's just not sure how it will be phrased. Will it be a question about decision-making, problem-solving, cross-cultural communication?

Yet the question isn't at all what she expected.

"Describe a past situation that left you feeling conflict between your own values and those of the U.N.," he asks. This man is definitely North African and wears a gele, a traditional African headwrap. Otherwise, his T-shirt and jeans are decidedly Western. His smile is wide enough to alert Dianna that he's faking it. He's heard of her past, and he doesn't want to hire her. Her heart cries out in grief, but she keeps an outward calm. He's questioning her integrity, perhaps even her morals. Might as well dive in.

"You must know that I felt I had little choice in Sudan."

"Perhaps you should have shared your concerns with your team members."

"I became ill shortly after I discovered the nature of the situation."

The man, named Mohammed, raises his eyebrow again, perhaps this time in disbelief. He shifts his body away from hers and places his finger in the air but holds back any scolding. "That is not precisely what I have heard."

She can feel perspiration bead her forehead, almost as if she's back in Africa on an interminable hot journey. Her mind flashes back, first to Khalil, then Biel, then the ride to the village where she became ill. She can almost literally feel the sun beating down on her hair. "And what exactly have you heard, Mohammed?" she asks with a stalwart gaze toward him, then to the entire group. Underneath, she's seething at the lack of training she'd gotten, the loner position they'd put her in, the lack of reconnaissance and research before they'd sent her into a militia base that was training child soldiers. She should be the one questioning them. She struggles not to frown.

"I was in a delicate, Catch-22 situation, a situation becoming all the more common. I assume you'd want to hire an expert who has had such an intractable experience and has learned from her mistakes, which I have done. It would never have happened if a child had not been involved." She brings herself up short before admitting she had loved Khalil.

"Why don't you tell us the entire story," says the human resources director, and the peacekeeper nods in anticipation.

It's the first time she's been asked to relay the story in detail, but she's almost numb from effort at this point, and so she does: the day Khalil appeared, his request to be taught, her discussions with Biel with a decided slant in her favor, her efforts to obtain refugee status for Khalil in Nairobi, and the full report she made upon her return.

"It was a child," says the peacekeeper. "A tiny child."

"I learned that all people are worth the effort," Dianna says. "He was one of the most vulnerable, but he was not in the most danger, per se."

"And you would handle it in what way in the future?" asks the mission director.

Dianna searches her heart and knows she'd handle exactly the same if it happened again. It would have been wrong, perhaps, and yet she wanted to rescue Khalil even now.

"I was rash in my actions," she says. "I would have followed the communication chain upwards. I would have sent word for my head of delegation to come for an investigative visit. I would not have left on any assignment Biel gave me until they arrived. I would have only taken up the matter with Biel if I had reinforcements from my team present. I would not have attempted to communicate with Khalil again."

She takes another deep breath because she can tell they are listening, that she is convincing them. "I would have realized he was just one more soul in a vast array of souls that all need our help. I would not have singled him out. Nor would I have if I'd enlisted team assistance. Acted according to U.N. protocol. Taken the appropriate steps."

She pauses and looks around the room. All eyes are on her but with looks of empathy, not disapproval.

"That is why I am requesting a less arduous position in Addis Ababa, where I will be a team member instead of a teacher. I would enjoy the camaraderie, brainstorming, and protection of a team. I will not ever allow this kind of circumstance to happen again. Never."

"Thank you," the human resources director says. "That's all we have for now. Thank you for your candor. We'll be in touch." She goes and opens the door, but her hand touches Dianna's shoulder as she escorts her out. "Good luck," she whispers when they reach the hallway.

But her whisper is overshadowed by one from the director of mission inside. "She scares me," he whispers, *sotto voce.*

She walks down the hall, revisiting the interview. Has she served enough penance as a translator? She figures she stands a 50/50 chance.

CHAPTER SEVENTEEN: CRISIS

December 17, 1992
New York City

A knock sounds at the door. Dianna throws down her pencil, thinking it's Leah again. When would Leah learn to take her belongings with her? "Damn it, Leah," she begins as she flings the door open. "You'd lose your head . . ."

A woman with chocolate skin and a long purple scarf stands there, holding a baby. She flinches and turns away as though Dianna is going to hit her. She may have heard her curse. She's exchanged "*Salaam Alaikums*" by the mailboxes with this woman. Dianna's admired her colorful flowing *julabias* and bracelets. Maybe she's come to visit. "I am sorry," the woman begins.

Then Dianna looks down at her baby. She can tell before the other woman utters a word that the baby has a fever. His face is red underneath his dark smooth skin, and his body is almost melting in sweat. The woman must have nobody to turn to but her.

"Come in," Dianna pulls the woman and child through the doorway and motions them to sit on her couch. "Can you speak English?" she asks.

Eyes round with fear, the woman tries to get words out, but instead, she utters a choking sound. She says something in what seems to be an African dialect, then a few words in Arabic, then mutters, "Yes—little."

Dianna touches her hand. "Don't be afraid," she says. Then she repeats it in French. Then in her rudimentary Arabic. The woman doesn't seem to understand that either. Dianna, for the millionth time, wishes she'd been able to take Arabic in school when she was conjugating French verbs. Maybe she wasn't saying it correctly. She knows *hello, good-bye,* and *thank you* from her time with Qasim, and a few simpler words from her time overseas, but speaking in sentences is another matter. But wishes aren't going to help this baby. Dianna fetches an ice-cold washcloth and lays it on the baby's forehead.

"Will he drink?" she asks. She makes a motion that reflects her words, bringing her hand up to her mouth and down again.

"*Na'am.*" The woman nods her head and frowns. "Yes."

The baby, despite such a high fever, is still responsive. He is listless, though, his eyes staring at the ceiling as though blind.

"No *visi ri.* No find *visi ri.*"

Dianna recognizes the name of the bitter shrub that most Sudanese claim works better than chloroquine for malaria. Its shoots bend to follow the sun. It does not grow here, and she's certain no American doctor has ever heard of it, or at least not in its natural form.

"No, they do not have it here," she explains in both English and

French, then says, *No have* in Arabic, shaking her head. "We need to take him to hospital." She makes the sound of a siren.

"No!" the woman shouts. "*Visi ri.*"

"Hospital," Dianna replies, her voice firm, almost rigid. She must convince this woman. Her baby could lapse into a coma if he doesn't get help.

She has no baby thermometer to determine how high his fever is. She cannot ask the woman if there have been convulsions. She'd never seen a thermometer in Sudan.

Just then, the baby's body goes limp, and his mother starts wailing—big mournful sobs that echo her desperation for her child, echoing years of similar despair.

Dianna shoots off the couch and dials 911. The woman rocks back and forth and removes prayer beads from her skirt pocket.

"911," comes a voice over the phone. "What is your emergency?"

The young mother begins to scream. How can the voice on the line be so calm when her own knees are shaking?

"I have a baby here, probably between one and two, who may be having febrile seizures. He is still breathing."

"What is your address, ma'am? We'll send someone out," the dispatcher says in a monotone.

She gives out the address twice. "Please hurry!"

The African woman looks up for a moment though she keeps rocking. "No doctor," she says, but this time with less vehemence.

Dianna is about to hang up, but the dispatcher begins to ask questions. "Has the baby had acetaminophen or ibuprofen?"

"I don't know," Dianna almost lets out a nervous giggle. What was the word in Arabic for ibuprofen?

"How long has the fever lasted?" the voice asks. Dianna looks over to see the baby's arms have started jerking.

"I don't know."

The voice heaves a heavy sigh. "Ma'am, I take it this is not your baby?"

"No!" Dianna answers. "This woman just showed up on my doorstep with her very ill child. I think she speaks Arabic, but she may speak Portuguese or even an African dialect. She doesn't speak French or English. Can you send someone who speaks Arabic to calm her down? She's very upset."

The woman kneels over her child, chanting.

"We'll do our best, ma'am." The phone clicks, and then Dianna hears the dial tone. She hangs up the phone, walks over to the woman, sits beside her, and puts her arm around her. The baby is alive for now.

CHAPTER EIGHTEEN: REFUGEES

That Night
New York City

The paramedics ring her bell without buzzing in downstairs. The ring sends both women dashing to the door, but the African woman gets there first and bars Dianna's way. "No, no!" she begs.

"It's the only way," Dianna explains and pushes the woman aside as gently as she would a tiny bird. She feels the woman's bones underneath her loose clothing. The woman puts her face in her hands and begins to sob again.

Two male paramedics enter the room and immediately go to the baby, checking his respiration and pulse. "Has he had a cold bath?" one asks. Dianna tells him he has not, hoping she is right. One of the workers bends over the child and caresses his face before he takes out more equipment. That gesture seems familiar. Has she seen him somewhere before? Then she notices he might be Mediterranean . . .

Hispanic, Italian, Israeli, Greek perhaps, or Arab. She goes to him and touches his arm. "Do you speak Arabic?" she asks.

"Yes," he replies. Again, that feeling of recognition shoots through her, but she cannot place where she would have seen this young man before. He places an electronic thermometer in the child's ear.

"This woman speaks Arabic, I believe." Dianna points toward the woman, who is cowering in the corner. "She is afraid, and I don't speak Arabic." She blushes because she wishes she did.

The emergency worker, whose head almost touches the top of Dianna's low ceiling, rises and strides with purpose over to the woman. Sitting on the edge of the couch, the woman puts her hands over her face in the same gesture she'd used with Dianna earlier, as though he might strike her. He begins to speak, and she brings her hands down from her face, and eventually, they rest in her lap. She stops crying and begins to respond to him.

The other two workers place a refrigerated stretcher under the child, start an I.V., and get ready to move him. Walkie Talkie voices fill every corner of the room as they exchange vitals and receive direction. "He's stable, but we'll have to take him in," the other worker, with shaggy blonde hair and a goatee, tells Dianna.

"Tell him to explain to the mother." Dianna points to the young man doing the translating.

He steps over to the other man, and they talk, the familiar one translating everything the other man says to the mother. She nods, sheds a few more tears, and nods again. The familiar man looks at Dianna and motions her over. "Can you follow us?" he asks. "She wants you to come. We're going to Mercy Hospital."

Dianna assents and retrieves her coat. *Never a dull moment. How did this happen when she thought she would be studying?*

She arrives at the hospital long after the ambulance, and she worries she has missed the emergency team. She's full of questions. Her stomach churns as she catches the white noise and stench of an emergency room at night. The last time she'd visited a hospital was when her mother was dying, more than a year ago. Yet it feels no different. Until she sees the E.M.T. She rushes into the emergency room reception area, and he's sitting there.

"My shift is over. I thought you might want to know what's wrong," he says, giving her a crooked little boy grin.

"Thank you! Thank you for being there. Thank God you were there to convince her." She extends her hand. "I'm Dianna Calloway."

"I'm Tariq el-Kafry." He extends his hand to meet hers. She steps back at the mention of the last name. Yet there must be many people with his last name after all.

"Are you alright?" he smiles. "You look as though you need to sit down. The baby will be fine. Just an untreated relapse of malaria. Really." When he says "really," she has no doubts. He says the word exactly as his father does.

"Why did she come to me?" Dianna asks. "Someone must have told her I worked in Africa."

"Sit down, please, Miss." Tariq points at the bright orange swivel chair beside him, and Dianna sinks into it, the room out of focus. "She's Sudanese," Tariq explains. "Your building receptionist told her you got back from Sudan recently."

"Yes," Dianna says, a response and a question in one. She pushes her hair back behind her ear, a nervous gesture. She's uncomfortable with this topic.

"She was the second wife of a prominent village elder," Tariq continues. "She is Arab; he is Dinka. He sent her here with the children to keep them safe."

"Children?" She's incredulous.

"Yes," Tariq says. "There are two older ones back in her apartment. They haven't been here very long. She didn't tell me until we got here. We've sent a couple of officers to pick them up and bring them here. The baby was probably starting to contract malaria before they arrived.

"The father was afraid they would be a target," Tariq continues. "They were both Muslim, but the difference in skin color . . ." He smooths his jacket and looks at the floor. "He was from an indigenous tribe. The only reason he knew Arabic was because he was a merchant and a farmer." He pauses, watching an elderly man being pushed by in a wheelchair. "For trade," he says, as though she doesn't completely understand, though she does. "Good luck for the baby," he laughs. "I don't speak any African languages."

"What will become of them?" Dianna asks, though she knows the question is redundant.

"She wants to go back," Tariq shifts his feet, looks in her eyes as though judging her character, and then back at his feet again. "She says she wants to change the color of her skin and the texture of her hair, so she can return home. She just wants to go back home." He shrugs.

"I guess that's what we all want."

"Not me!" Tariq says a little too loudly, and people lift their chins off their chests to see the commotion.

"I've seen enough of 'home,'" he continues. "Although my mother's there." His eyes look bright with something that might be fear but also might be anger.

"You've seen too much war, I suspect." Dianna looks directly into his eyes, this son of the man she used to love. He is real, standing there before her.

"If you've been in Sudan, you must know. I don't hold much hope for our part of the world."

"What brought you here?" Dianna asks.

"Medical school, and my father." He laughs, but it comes out tinny and sarcastic. "Although my father isn't here any longer."

"I believe I know your father," Dianna says. "Qasim el-Kafry?" She stuffs her hands down in her coat pockets, so deep she thinks she might rip the seams.

"No, you're kidding!" Tariq exclaims, his eyes growing so wide the brown irises seem to almost touch their corners. He's probably thinking he said too much. "How do you know my father?"

Dianna smiles. It's a difficult question to answer, especially to Tariq. "We're friends," she says simply. "But I haven't seen him in a while."

"Neither have I." Tariq extends his hand once more. "What did you say your name was? I am so glad to know you."

"Dianna Calloway." She looks at this young man, who looks nothing like his father, but whose mannerisms echo every movement her memory holds dear. He has wavy hair, long skinny arms, a prominent nose, straight teeth like a strand of shiny pearls, and he is tall, oh, so tall. Even when they are seated, she must look up to meet his gaze, his only feature reminiscent of Qasim. His eyes are rippling black orbs of intelligence and wit and sadness.

He looks down for a moment as though wondering what to say. "My father spoke of you. I am sure of it. You knew him when I was young, yes?"

"Will you tell him I'd like to say 'hello' if he's ever in town?" Qasim spoke of her to him!

"Sure, I'm certain he'll be excited we met."

"Only if he has time, of course. I know how busy he gets."

"I'm sure he will make the time. As I said, he has spoken of you. I don't know when he'll get here, though. At the moment, he is in Eastern Europe." He looks down at the floor when he says this, as his father would have done, as though he is finding Europe on a map.

"Oh," Dianna replies. He's keeping something from her. "Interesting. I never saw him being in that part of the world. But with the dissolution of the Soviet Union, I guess it makes sense. He's still with the U.N.?" No wonder she'd been unable to find him. He hadn't been sent on the mission he originally thought he had received.

"Oh, yes," Tariq rolls his eyes. "*That* will be the day when he leaves. They'll have to carry him out in a coffin." They have a good laugh, and Dianna goes back with him to check on her new neighbors.

"Aisha." The woman points at her chest and bows. She puts her hand on her sleeping boy's head and smiles. "Ibrahim."

"Dianna," she answers and points at her own chest.

Aisha's older children have joined them, and she points at them and says their names, but Dianna's pulse is so loud and her mind so full, she won't remember their names. A child almost died. She helped save his life. And somehow, now they were all connected with Tariq. Qasim's son.

Aisha says something to Tariq, and he turns again to Dianna. "She says many thanks for your generosity. May Allah be good to you. Thanks to you, her boy will live. May you and your husband have many offspring."

"Thank you." Dianna places her hand on her heart. "Please tell her I have no husband but am grateful for her well wishes."

After Tariq stops chatting with her, the woman rises and kisses Dianna on both cheeks, repeating *thank you* over and over, and Dianna returns her kisses. "No. Not just me. Tariq and the other emergency team members helped, too."

She suddenly realizes how exhausted she is and how much more work must be finished before sunrise. "I need to go home." She pulls some paper out of her purse and scribbles her phone number twice in big, bold numerals. She gives one slip of paper to Aisha, who offers hers in turn, the other to Tariq. "Please," she says, and her voice breaks. "Please stay in touch."

She walks to the swinging E.R. door and turns back. They're both watching her leave. She waves goodbye. "I'll check in on your family tomorrow," she tells Aisha, and Tariq translates.

"I'll be in touch," he calls behind Dianna as the door swings shut.

CHAPTER NINETEEN: FRIENDSHIP

January 12, 1993
New York City

Mirembe arrives with little advance notice the day before her original arrival date. She's staying with Dianna while on a business trip to the U.N. Instead of stocking her empty fridge, Dianna decides to take her out for a nice Italian dinner.

"I'm looking forward to our conversation," Dianna says. "We never had time before. I'd love to hear all the news."

Mirembe has a hearty appetite. Dianna's used to enough food now, but she'd wolfed down her first full meal back in the States. It was as though she was eating food cooked for gods. It had tasted that good. She's glad she can nurture Mirembe.

"Thank you! Delicious!" Mirembe rubs her belly. "Not just for the meal. For seeing me. Especially after the way my country treated you."

"I thought that was how they treated all *khawajas.*" Dianna signals to the server to bring a carafe of red wine.

"Oh, you are probably correct. I would still appreciate your accepting my apology. You see, I know better, having spent some time in the U.K. and here."

"You lived here?"

"Not lived, exactly. I studied here for a year. I love the hustle and bustle. People here are friendly. So many of my people do not understand that. They know only what the papers and televisions show them."

"Thank you." Dianna feels herself soften.

"I wanted to help you, but I would have risked my life."

"I figured so."

"You did?" Now it's Mirembe's turn to be surprised. "Did you know why?"

"I did not. I could tell you had reason to keep your silence, though."

"The same reason I am here."

"And that is . . . ?"

"I will tell you a story," Mirembe says, in true African style. "There was once a fair maiden . . ."

Dianna assumes the fair maiden was Mirembe.

"She was the beauty of her tribe. She was attracted to its dashing young future leader. She did not hang the sun or moon in the sky for him, but after a time, the leader began to show her favor. He saw she received an education. There was talk in her village that the two would be paired."

"And were they?" Dianna takes another sip of her wine.

"No. The young man came back from England with his bride."

"Oh no. I am sorry." She's starting to comprehend the energy she felt at camp between Mirembe and Biel. Respect. Disappointment. Trust also? They knew what the other would do because of their lifelong connection.

"Oh no, do not apologize! He was a man full of ego. I am well in my soul without him."

"I can understand that."

"He turned down a shadowed path."

"Yes."

Mirembe shifts in her seat, probably exhausted from days of travel, but she continues. "I have decided to leave and stop following him," she almost whispers.

"Where shall you go?"

"I was hoping here." Mirembe's voice breaks. "I am afraid of what he will do to me, to my people, if I leave, if I do not follow. My life is certainly at risk just because I came here briefly. Yet my country is a dangerous place on all fronts. If I do not get my family away, they may all die. The U.N. has agreed to help me."

"That's wonderful news!"

"Yes. But I cannot bring Khalil."

"Khalil?" Dianna needs her to repeat the name. Did she hear correctly?

"Yes. He is the son of the woman Biel married, the one he brought to Sudan, the one who left Biel and Khalil to return to London only months before you arrived."

What a fool she's been, thinking Biel was abusing Khalil when he'd been trying to protect him. She's seen only darkness in the man because of his young troops. True, he was anything but an angel. War can make men evil. At least he cared about his son. "He sent her back?"

"Not really. It was more that she left them. Biel did not want their son to be with her if she was not with Biel. He wanted them all to be together."

Of course, he would want his children with him, but it must be terrible for the mother.

"Biel has had two attempts on his life. The first from another tribal leader. The second from one of his own men. He feared that if he let Khalil remain with him, bandits could kidnap him. So, with a heavy heart, he sent me to return Khalil back to his mother. Then I came to see you."

"Thank you, Mirembe, for telling me all this."

"I needed to. I wanted to the last time we met, at the delegation. But I was being watched."

"By whom?"

Mirembe does not answer. "You care for my people, Dianna. You think you hide your feelings. But you do not. You are a kind person. It is I who must thank you if none of my countrymen will." Mirembe puts her hand over Dianna's.

"You are welcome to stay for as long as you need, Mirembe."

"I thank you for that, too. But just the night will do. I wanted to give you this message. Because I promised. I do not break my promises."

"Who did you promise?"

"Khalil. He wanted you to know he was fine for the time being." With that, Mirembe yawns, and they head back for a night of restless sleep. Khalil is alive. Khalil is fine. Khalil is with his mother. How impetuous and misguided she's been.

And yet, her heart aches. She'll never see him again.

CHAPTER TWENTY: CASUALTIES

February 26, 1993
New York City

Dianna looks over the top of the newspaper she's reading. Aisha's not there yet. She can keep reading. Some good news for a change to compare with all the violence.

The day is nippy but sunny. The steps of the Met are like a café in Paris without the beverages, smoke, and dogs. A café without coffee . . . it literally takes the meaning out of the word. The big dogs here are taking walks, not sitting on chairs. The man over there, stripped down to shorts and a sleeveless sweatshirt, in forty-degree weather no less, is jogging with a yellow lab, and even the lady in the hot pink hat is walking a German shepherd . . . labs and shepherds, not poodles and Pekinese.

She misses Europe and Africa. Aisha reminds her of Africa, her life interrupted. She wants to go back. This job in Addis fell through, and it may have been Biel's doing. Or Mirembe's even. Though they say another may open up in a few months. She's not one to give up. She's kept applying. And maybe she's only imagining people gossiping about her past performance behind her back.

The two women embrace, the children gather around, and they begin their trek toward the local deli. Their conversations have more flow now. Aisha is teaching Dianna Arabic, and Dianna is teaching Aisha English. She's starting to look forward to spending the weekends with the children.

"It is good to meet you," Aisha says.

She means "see," of course. Yet the rest of the sentence is perfect. "It is good to *see* you, too," Dianna replies.

"My husband writes."

"Yes?"

"He bids hello. He thanks you."

"Oh, I thank him for my new friends." Dianna feels a real smile, the first since she left Africa, pull at her mouth. She lets it go, big and wide.

Aisha does likewise. She reaches out and grips Dianna's hand, and they remain that way. What would she have done without this family as she transitioned back to her old, mundane life? Aisha's voice is full of Africa, her children, a memory of Khalil. She has taken Dianna's mind off Qasim. It's not that she can ever forget Africa, Khalil, especially not Qasim. She knows that. Yet, this friendship, full of unconditional love, safe here in her homeland, has gauzed the wounds she carries with her from others she's loved.

Sirens meet them in the street, more sirens than the usual commotion.

It is colder today than a few days ago, but the sky has that blue crystal quality that is almost surreal. Pedestrians look around; something is not right. A man in a navy overcoat walks by, holding a cell phone. Two women race by, probably late getting back from lunch. A bicycle rider whizzes past.

Aisha's children are beautiful, with bright eyes and soulful smiles, and Dianna enjoys being with them and caring for them. Her make-believe family. What would it have been like to have a child? Qasim's child?

Aisha shivers as they enter the warm deli. Dianna likes the deli because she can escape cigarette smokers inside. People are still puffing away in Africa and Europe, where Dianna used to hide in a museum—any museum—just to get away from the smoke. She gives the man on the opposite side of the steps a look of disapproval as he lights up as they enter the deli. She rubs her eyes to get the stinging smoke out. Aisha doesn't notice.

She orders her usual, a tuna on rye with mustard, and Aisha follows her lead, ordering two more for the children to split. The children smell their sandwiches, then dig in.

"You return Africa?" Aisha asks. Her eyes are wide with concern. She knows Dianna has continued applying for other overseas jobs but has not gotten call-back interviews.

"Probably not." Dianna shrugs. "Not yet." She longs to go, but Africa may not want her. It may spit her out like it did before.

"*In'shallah*," Aisha says. "You will go. Africa waits."

"From your mouth to Allah's ear."

There's a television inside, and the lunchtime news is on. Dianna's begun to get media fatigue. There have been race riots in Crown Heights the same year as the war in the Gulf, the race riots in Los Angeles last year, and across the ocean, ethnic purges rage in what used to be Yugoslavia. Most everyone has forgotten the starvation and war in Sudan, in Ethiopia, and no one cares that countries on the Congo River are on the verge of flaring up. Who needs theft and murder when people feel they can act out their aggression by raping, pillaging, and killing at will? New York's almost eight-million residents now speak over ninety languages. They'd better learn to get along fast.

She points at the screen and asks Aisha if she understands, but Aisha shrugs. She points at her ear to show she doesn't yet understand the commentary. But she does understand the images. "War," she says and shrugs again. She knows that word, probably in several languages.

The kids laugh and sing, happy to have their bellies full and their foreheads cooler, malaria-free. This must seem like Paradise to them, but she can tell it is not so to Aisha. She picks at her food with the tip of her fork. They finish eating in silence, preferring to listen to the children's laughter and music.

"You miss home?" Dianna asks.

"Yes, much. Better for children here."

"I miss it, too." They'll always be straddling oceans, longing for one continent while living in the other.

"You not like here?" Aisha has a look of curious shock.

"I like it okay," Dianna says, slicing the sandwich in half with a plastic knife.

"Much food."

"Yes," Dianna agrees. "So many choices. Too many choices."

Food, food everywhere, but for some, not a bite to eat. She wants to tell Aisha her family had been on food stamps before she began working, but she knows she won't understand with the language barrier.

"You not have husband? Never?" Aisha asks and blushes. It's a forward question, but she's held off asking for a long time.

"No. There were two men I loved. I might have married one."

"I find him for you."

Dianna laughs. "Thank you, but it's not that easy here."

Aisha frowns. She hasn't understood.

"To find a husband, I mean."

Aisha's smile is shrewd. "I find you husband."

She almost believes her. But then Aisha can't even join her husband because of all these wars. "Go?" Dianna motions. She throws away their trash and hugs her new friend goodbye. They head out to a street full of flashing lights and sirens. Streets blocked in every direction.

Heading back to the office, Dianna goes up to the line of cabs that always line up outside her building. "What's going on?" she asks a cabbie in a purple turban. She can hear his radio blaring.

"World Trade Center's been bombed," he says. "Lots of casualties. Climb in. Listen."

Dianna slips into the front seat. "Can I pay you?" she asks, but he brushes her off as though he's offended.

The radio announcer's voice comes through with a practiced Manhattan cadence. Dianna can tell she is not from the city originally.

Today at 12:18 p.m., a bomb resonated in the garage of Tower One of the World Trade Center, killing five and injuring scores more.

The explosion ripped through three floors of concrete, scattering ash and debris, trapping thousands of office workers, unsure if evacuation was necessary. "It felt like an airplane hit the building," said an eyewitness. Terrorism is being investigated.

"So, it's finally here," Dianna mumbles.

The cabbie turns to her with a baffled expression. "You want to go somewhere, Miss?"

"No, thanks for your kindness," Dianna replies. She leaves five dollars in the seat. She heads back inside to her day's translations.

CHAPTER TWENTY-ONE: SAFE HAVEN

April 14, 1993
New York City

Dianna almost forgets about Tariq and his promise. He is his father's son, after all. Plus, she's used to empty promises, and every time she thinks of him, she wonders where Qasim is, and a longing begins to unfold that she can't contain. And she must. Because he is somewhere not with her. So, she runs.

She pulls on her jogging suit to head toward Central Park. The first tree blossoms fall around her as she moves forward. She plans to buy some tulips for her table when she returns. Aisha, her children, Sophia, and Leah are coming to dinner tonight. Dianna will serve kabobs, tabbouleh, and buy some stuffed grape leaves, but she plans to have apple pie for dessert. Apple pie with Arabic coffee. She wants to make Aisha and her family feel at home.

She lays out the ingredients she has on her counter to ensure one trip to the market is all that's necessary, all the while watching some sort of old Western re-run, probably the only one ever made without John Wayne. One of the cowboys is Asian. The costume designer and director granted the poor actor a cowboy hat and a horse but made him wear a pigtail. He seems to be the story's hero; however, he carries a buxom brunette over a small canyon, firing at their pursuers, who are dropping like flies. He gets the heroine (although Dianna cannot see why a fainting, screaming woman is deemed a heroine) to safety.

The phone rings, and she picks it up with a casual hello. She figures it is Leah, asking what she can bring.

"Shame on you!" comes the voice from the other end of the line. "Shame for not staying in touch!"

It is so good to hear his voice, but his words jar her soul. "Hello, Qasim," she says. "Where are you? How could I stay in touch if you didn't tell me where you were going? I tried to call you, but your number was disconnected."

He ignores her rebuke. "I am in Budapest." His voice is light. He must want to tease her, not annoy her, but his greeting still stings.

"Do you still talk to Sophia? Tell her I am in her hometown." His voice is very loud, as though he's speaking over static even though there is none.

"I will." Dianna reaches up and wishes she had a cord to twirl while she talks, but she bought a cordless phone just last weekend.

"I can see the Danube from my window. I'm on the hilltop; I can see almost every bridge. It's almost as if I could reach out and touch them. The river is flowing, though they tell me it can still be frozen this time of year. Come join me. Don't you want to see Budapest with me?"

"You know I can't come to Budapest spontaneously, Qasim. I'm not Samantha in *Bewitched*." She raises her eyebrow in consternation and counts to ten. He can be so maddening.

"What do you mean?" He sounds amused. "I am extending an invitation, a gentlemanly gesture. Chivalrous, even."

She's sure he's never watched American TV sitcoms of the 1960s and almost forgives him. Then she says, amazed at how calm and firm her voice sounds, "No. You cannot do this to me anymore. Stop turning my words on edge to make them your own."

"Again, I thought of you. I wanted you here by my side, Dianna. That is all." His voice is sober.

"And when I arrive, will you be there for me? Will you let me be there for you?"

"Come on, Dianna, that kidney infection was a long time ago. A speck of dust."

That wasn't total truth. He'd been quite ill. She'd wanted to go to him, thought he could be near death. And he wouldn't let her. "You always expect me to see things your way. When will you begin to try to see things my way? That speck of dust for you was a world of abandonment to me."

"Who was abandoning whom, Dianna?"

"Don't you try to weasel your way out of this conversation."

The silence is red hot, so Dianna can tell he has not hung up the phone at first, but then she begins to wonder as the silence cools. "Are you still there? I am glad you called."

"Of course, I am. I am not rude enough to hang up on you. What kind of person do you think I am?"

She knows he's chiding her while he is pumping himself up. She hung up on him years ago. "Stop it. Just stop it," she says. "You have a way of doling out blame, and I have a way of accepting it. Why can we not meet halfway? True equals would be building one another up instead of tearing each other down. My equal would come from a place of abundance, not lack."

Qasim sighs. "Why must we always argue? Who said I thought myself superior to you? Would I invite you if I did not want to see you?"

"No," Dianna replies. "No." She will not say *mea culpa*. So, she counts silently to twenty in French. Then says, "I wanted to thank you for getting me out of hot water in Nairobi. I had no idea how dangerous it was that day. I thought you were overreacting until I heard about the *mujahedin* locating in Nairobi and Mombasa once I arrived back here."

"You're welcome." His tone conveys more than his words. His voice is like a love poem, full of melody and rhythm, asking for forgiveness, not praise. *She should thank him more often.*

"I owe you one," she says in a tone to match his.

"Tariq told me about the baby—how you saved its life," he continues. His voice becomes soft, far away.

"Oh no, that was Tariq and the other rescue workers. You must be so proud of him." Dianna smiles as she thinks of Baby Ibrahim, of how he is alive, still here with his family, because of Tariq.

"Yes, indeed, I am." He pauses, and she can hear his soft breath. She is ready to speak when he repeats, "Shame on you, Dianna, really! Not telling me you were back in New York."

She smiles at the way he pronounces "really," how she used to tease him about it: how the "r" dances, how the word rhymes with "steely," instead of "silly." She can picture him there, his face part irony, part dictatorial. It feels familiar and frustrating, but forgivable. She cares for him despite their past, because of their past, and for what he knows of her past. She still wants to know more about him, yes, but if she does not find out, she can be at peace. She doesn't feel quite as much on the examining stand as she once did. She sits and pulls her legs close to her chest.

No, she will not let him in, not yet. He is nowhere near her, and he just shamed her.

"How was I to find you? Even if I am in New York, you're in Hungary," she states, her voice patient, as though she is speaking to one of Aisha's children. Her smile spreads as she listens to his silence.

"I—I tried," he stammers, then picks up his smooth tone again. "I know," he says with simplicity. "We are both bad at staying in touch, I suppose."

She feels her blood warm inside as she hears these words. They would not have been possible even a few years ago.

"It was nice of you to call me from overseas. You didn't have to do that."

"I wanted to," he says. There is another pause. "I mean it." She notices how clear his English has become, how his words are crisp and distinct.

"I want to see you. It may not be for a time, unless you can come here."

"I'm not sure I can afford it. Why don't you come to New York?"

Her mind turns to getting dinner ready, buying flowers for her centerpiece. The sun beckons her outside, and she thinks of those tulips swaying in the wind. She cannot let him linger, for that would make her miss him. Then she might even get on a plane to Budapest tomorrow.

She is ready to say she wishes he were there with her for her little dinner party but hears a beep on the other end of the phone. "Do you have another call?" she asks.

"No, it's my secretary buzzing me," he says. "I shall call as soon as I know when I will be there. It was so very good to hear your voice." He hangs up before she can answer.

CHAPTER TWENTY-TWO: ANTIQUITIES

June 11, 1993
New York City

When she needs to think, Dianna always ends up in the same place, no matter how far she wanders: the old Egyptian exhibit. Even the mummies' threads need some stitching, and she always sees something she's never seen before.

Today she is here because she needs to decide, and Sophia has said she'd help her sort through her list of pros and cons. She's finally been offered an assignment in Ethiopia. It is a good assignment, a development position instead of one amid open conflict. It is time to leave the limbo of the translations department, where she is simply the receptacle for other people's words, just like the faience vessel over there. She needs her own words, her own life.

She walks over to the viewing case containing the faience vessel so dear to her, more beautiful in its ancient repose than ever. The top of the bowl has human legs etched into it, something she has never noticed before. Funny how you can look at something and only see the parts of it you want to see, until you are ready.

She moves on to the next viewing case, standing transfixed in front of a necklace that belonged to, and was buried with, an Egyptian princess, full of golds and blues and ambers. The necklace is a collection of symbols for new life: the sun, cobra tails, falcons, scarabs, and of course, ankhs.

Her thoughts drift to her decision once again. She came back to her old way of life once; she's even improved upon it in ways. She can do it again. She sees her reflection in the glass pane, her frown an etched thought hovering over the falcon. She looks up higher and startles. In the murky reflection, a face peers over her right shoulder. The person has been so quiet she has not heard him approach. At first, she thinks it is a guard, but then he speaks.

"Your colleague Sophia told me you would be here," Qasim says, his voice measured. She can catch a waft of his cologne as he moves closer, a different scent, not as strong as it used to be. She stares through the pane, still not turning around.

"I can't believe it's you," she says finally. "The last time I spoke to you was almost two months ago."

He puts his hand on her shoulder and turns her to face him. "I'm sorry I couldn't come sooner. I had work that had to be done."

"I know. You always do."

"I'm here now."

"For a while."

"For a while," he answers, a trace of remorse in his voice.

He kisses her mouth, and she returns the kiss. It is a soft kiss of recognition and remembrance. She also feels its loss and anxiety. She pulls away and looks at him, up and down, counting the changes. The hair on his temples and sideburns has gone completely gray. Puffy circles surround his black-brown eyes, showing through his dark tan. Reading glasses perch on his forehead like they are a part of him. He still dresses well: tailored navy jacket, tweedy gray pants, a tie with geometry.

"How long has it been?" she asks.

"Ten, no eleven, years. We go back a long, long way, you and I."

"No, I meant since we last saw one another in Nairobi." She realizes he is referring to how long they have known each other, not how long since their last meeting. "How could that many years have passed since we first met?"

"The blink of an eye for those who've cared about each other."

She shakes her head "no." Time spent apart was different than spent together. He doesn't seem to understand this simple fact.

He reaches for her hand. "Come with me. I want to show you something." She feels the grip of his tapered, reassuring fingers around her own. Despite his physical changes, his hand still feels like home. They walk through several rooms until they are in the Islamic wing. The room is full of patterns—blue and green tile flowers, wooden and ivory mosaic stars, red and bronze knotted carpet wool. Everything, even the Arabic writing in some of the designs, forms a small pattern that is part of the whole. The exhibit lights cast shadow patterns on the floor.

"Here." He points to a painting in the far-left corner. "This is a picture of my favorite story from the Qur'an."

She recognizes it immediately as Jonah. He emerges from the whale's mouth. Actually, it is some other sort of big fish. The angel who hands Jonah his clothes is beautiful, with intricate patterns on his, or perhaps it is her, green, red, and gold wings. Vegetation sprouts up from all corners of the canvas, and a vine sprouts up out of Jonah's head.

"Why is the angel handing him his clothes?"

"To show that we depend on God's will for everything," Qasim almost whispers. "In' shallah."

Dianna racks her brain for what she knows about Jonah after the whale spat him out. He was a prophet, but what else? "I think Jonah had his own book in our Bible."

"Really?" he says. "Interesting." He puts his arm around her, still gazing at the picture.

"Why do you love this story so?" she nestles in his arm, not wanting to think about what will happen next.

"The story is about forgiveness."

She turns her head and looks into his eyes, still that ebony shining in them, trying to see if there is more he cannot say. There is, and she knows if she asks right now, he will not tell her, that he might even walk away. So, she is silent.

"Is it not beautiful?" he asks.

"Very," she replies and rubs her hair against his chin.

• • •

Today, a decade after their first shared meal, they have lunch in

Manhattan. Instead of a yuppie pizza place, they walk to a deli that serves fast-food sushi. Qasim looks Dianna up and down as they stand in the long line of lunch-hour workers. She should have polished her shoes.

"You're looking very tall and thin," Qasim says. His hand slips through hers.

"Thanks, it's good to see you. I suppose I have Tariq to thank." She feels her face redden.

"You do."

"He is so handsome and so true."

He smiles, and she can see his pride resonate. "Yes, he is." Then his smile fades, and the crease above his nose gets deeper. "I hope he will do well."

"Why wouldn't he?"

Qasim heaves a long sigh and pulls his jacket sleeves down over his cufflinks. "You wouldn't understand, Dianna."

"Try me. I have met him now, after all. He seems to be making his way." She reaches out and puts her hand over his.

"Tariq keeps changing his mind." His smile changes to a frown and back to a smile again. "He should be finished with pre-med by now. And why is he working his way through school? He doesn't need to do that. I've tried to arrange meetings with eligible young women, but he will have none of it. For all I know, he doesn't date at all. And he tells me nothing. He tells his mother nothing."

"Places influence you. He lives here now. He is young, also." They are making their selections, and she picks up a container labeled "medley."

"What does that have to do with his familial responsibility? He is my only son!"

"Everybody says language, culture, or religion make a person. I beg to differ. I can't recall the military base where I was born. We left there before I turned two. Yet I take that 'place' with me wherever I go because I learned to talk there. And I take the next base I lived. And the next city, Chicago. And the next, Memphis. African cities and villages, too. We take our geography with us; we carry each piece of it to our next home like a portable scrapbook. We're a product of all the places we've lived."

"And you, Dianna, you haven't stayed American?" Qasim turns his entire body away from her.

She steps back a notch. "Not entirely. But I have America in me, the North and South. You do, too, Qasim. You can't expect him to stay purely Lebanese any more than you did."

"You do have a point."

"I think we stay basically who we are, no matter where we go, but we add new dimensions along the way. I have the dirt roads of the Carolinas here, the deserts and savannahs of Sudan there, Victoria Falls here, and the snow-capped Alps here." Dianna points to an elbow, another elbow, a knee, another knee, another elbow. "And all the people and places in between.

I wonder if I hadn't met you, if I'd have stayed satisfied with my lot in life. I looked at you, and I saw, immediately, what was possible. The irony was that, though you showed me, you couldn't help me achieve it."

Qasim pays the cashier, says nothing, and keeps his eyes to the floor as they carry their sushi to a crowded table. He turns up his nose at the crumbs left behind, and they stand waiting for another table to open up. "I am sorry, sweetie. I tried." He squints his eyes as though he is looking into the distance. "I suppose I see what you mean," he finally answers.

"I thank you for what you did give me, Qasim."

"Don't give credit where credit isn't due, Dianna. You wouldn't let me help you. And perhaps I wasn't able to help you . . . then. Yet, I so want to help Tariq. I so want Tariq to have the life I didn't have."

"Then let him live his life, Qasim," she says when they find a free, cleaner table. "He'll find his way. You can't expect him to be just another boy from Beirut. Not in these times. Not with you as his father."

Qasim shakes his head, first slowly, then with vehemence. He watches people come and go. He's always people-watched, just like her. Especially if he's trying to find words. "I have learned it matters not where we live; we must fulfill the expectations of our cultures. I wish it weren't so, but it is."

"Are freedom and Islam really at odds?" Dianna flinches, ready for a violent counterattack, a reflex from her childhood. She's asked a bold question, too familiar for someone she's no longer intimate with.

Yet looking up, all she sees in Qasim—in his eyes, his shoulders, even his hands resting on the tips of his knees—is a certain wistful pondering. In the cacophony of the restaurant, all seems suddenly still. Dianna can hear her watch ticking. She wants to look at her wrist but is afraid she will remind Qasim he must go. They're not even pretending to pick at their food.

Finally, deliberately, he says, "Dianna, sweetie, no one ever talks to me like that."

She sucks in air.

She lets it out again as he continues. "I'm not able to speak like this with anyone but you. I don't have the answer to that question, though. I'll leave it to the next generation. This I do know because you taught me. Freedom is not wrong. Love is not wrong."

For one brief second, she thinks he might continue, about their past, about a possible future. Yet he changes the subject quickly, as though he has not just spoken those words, and her hopes fall like petals from a flower in the fall. "You're a translator now. Is that correct?" he asks.

"Yes, though I'd rather be in the field. I'm just taking a break of sorts. I needed to be here for my family for a time, and I needed the rest from all the global intrigue." Dianna raises her eyebrow.

"Yes, family comes first."

"I'll go back with reinforcements soon enough; in fact, I've been offered a position in Ethiopia. I learned in Sudan I must go back to Africa with new insight and strategy. So, it's important that I figure out another way to help the most vulnerable before I return."

Qasim smiles a knowing smile. "That's the word of the business now, 'vulnerable.'"

She can tell he's proud of her while simultaneously sad they can't make more of a difference. "I am not in the States for very long myself," he says.

Dianna dips her shrimp roll into a sauce. She thinks she likes the sauce better than the sushi.

Qasim looks at her unenthusiastic expression and chuckles. "I would have rather had pizza, too." She's surprised, both that he remembers the pizza place they frequented and that he has read her thoughts.

"Will you go back to Eastern Europe?" she asks. She pictures him there on the Charles Bridge in Prague, perhaps, a place she has seen only on a postcard.

"No," he says and hesitates. He runs his index finger along her jaw line, then around the tips of her fingernails. "They want me back in my part of the world. They say my experience is much needed there." He looks up into her eyes, back down again, moves his finger back and forth, back and forth. His eyes become moist, and hers do, too.

"So, you're going back to Lebanon?" Dianna asks, trying to put optimistic inquisitiveness into a voice on the verge of breaking. "It seems you only just left there."

"I think, actually, they will send me to the Gulf. Maybe Oman."

How far away! Two or three flight connections instead of a direct flight from here. Who knows how many connections from Ethiopia? The old sadness pricks at her insides, and she crosses her arms over her waist. She thinks he notices her sorrow. She wouldn't mind if he did.

They stare at each other for several minutes. A couple of men sit next to them. Too close. Their voices carry across the room, discussing the latest sports news.

"Do they televise sports in Oman?" she asks and starts to laugh and then cry.

"Of course," he says, and his eyes have that impatient professor look she knows so well. Yet he's noticed she'll miss him. She hopes he hasn't noticed she wants to entreat him to stay with her. It wouldn't be fair to ask before she's sure she truly wants him to remain. When she's leaving for Ethiopia.

The cashier leaves her post and starts to wipe off the tables. She picks up Dianna's plate, which still has two pieces of untouched sushi, and throws it in the garbage, never saying a word.

Qasim looks perturbed at the rude gesture and the interruption.

"I think you should stay here, Dianna. Your country needs people like you."

"No one tells me what to do," she says, and he grimaces. There, she's wounded him, just as he's done her. Why can't they both just stay here and love each other? Why is it always work when love is what the world needs?

He twirls his napkin round and round before setting it on the table.

"Quite a nice table decoration," Dianna jokes. She knows him well enough to know he has had enough seriousness.

"I thought you'd like it," he retorts.

"I'm going to Addis."

"Addis isn't very safe right now," he says.

She blinks. "Seems I've heard this pronouncement from you before. And what place is?"

They are silent again until he says, "If you go to Addis, will you come visit me in Oman?"

"Of course, I will. I would do that with an advance invitation even if I was here."

"You didn't before. You wouldn't come to Budapest."

"I wasn't ready. You weren't ready. How long were you even

visiting Hungary? You need to give me time to pack first." She doesn't say she is thinking they might finally be ready. Perhaps not for commitment. Perhaps that is not what life has meant for them to pursue, maybe a simple love, a friendship.

"I will give you notice," Qasim agrees, and cups his hand over hers, then takes it away as quickly.

Perhaps he thinks they're still not ready. "Are you going to stay at this forever?" Dianna asks, hoping she has collected herself enough to discuss this like an adult. If he doesn't keep working, he may never pass through the United States again. Yet his thin frame, thinner than a few months ago, and the crisscross lines around his eyes, show the time he has spent on U.N. missions of late has not been kind to him. Near fifty, but he looks a decade older. How much longer can he push himself?

"Come now, Dianna," he says, and his eyes dance with what might be sarcasm or sincerity. "Nothing lasts forever. We both know that."

"I'd love for you to come over for dinner while you're here," she says.

"I accept." He gets up quickly, upsetting his flimsy chair, and comes and holds her, showers her with exuberant kisses.

"What about tonight?"

Chapter Twenty-three: Reunion

That Night

"This is like old times," Qasim says when she opens the door and invites him into her apartment. He sniffs the air. "Is that thyme I smell? It smells like *manakish*, our little thyme pizzas back home! What did you make me for the dinner I enjoyed so much?"

Dianna cannot remember. That was an era of her life when she did not want to think about food, when she fought with it, and it usually won. "It was so long ago," she murmurs.

"No, no, I remember." He smiles. "I remember everything." He takes off his overcoat, throws it on her couch, and strides around the room, rubbing his hands together. "Let me see: steak and potatoes, like a true American, and hummus and eggplant with garlic and cinnamon, like a true Arab. And you had sprinkled thyme on the bread you served."

"Well, you're getting two of those tonight." She smiles. "The bread and the eggplant dish."

185

"My favorite! *Batinjaan bi zayt.* I can't wait."

"You must. Everything is still in the oven." She starts to go to the refrigerator to offer him a drink.

"Give me the tour," he says, throwing his arms around her.

She wiggles free. "How can I give you the tour or feed you if I can't move?" She laughs.

"Right. The tour." He looks chastened. How would he react if she told him to go stand in the corner? Her heart opens a crack and then another, letting feeling for him drip in like a much-needed transfusion; he is trying so hard.

"This is the living room," she says. "This is my couch. These are my cushions. I covered them myself, except this one. It came from Africa." The cushion is earthen in color and has a few fake jewels sewn into the fabric: olives, rusts, and golds.

"I can tell," he murmurs. "Beautiful."

"This is my card table." She laughs and pulls up the elegant lace tablecloth, which had been her mother's, to show the rickety table underneath. "I was thinking of getting a cat, but I never know if I'll stay or not."

"I know, I know."

"That's my kitchen, such as it is, kind of tiny, but I painted it cheery yellow."

"Yellow for creativity." He pulls her to him again. "Dianna, your hairstyle is very becoming," he says. "Really."

Dianna touches her hair, blunt from last week's trim. "Thanks." She means it.

"Come here." She wants to show him her photo albums, especially the one from Sudan. She pulls him down on the sofa beside her and runs her fingers over the creases in his forehead. He makes a noise, perhaps a moan, but he catches himself. "Down, boy," she says, with a half-hearted push away.

The vulnerable little-boy-look shows up on his face again for a moment, the look he must have given his mother when she caught him doing something he shouldn't. Here in America, it would be stealing from the cookie jar. What would it have been in Beirut? Her imagination cannot go there. Instead, it settles on the desolate little hut she had in Sudan.

"Here," she says. "This is me in front of the camp where I taught reading."

"You taught reading? In English?"

"Yes, English materials were all they equipped me with."

"They ought to fix that."

"Yes, they should, but they don't." She flips the page. No sense in getting into a discussion about work. "These are my children," she says and then thinks again. "They don't look much like children, do they? More like tiny adults."

"Yes." He swallows hard and turns the page.

"Who is this?" He points to one of the photographs.

"Oh, that is Khalil." She traces the fingertips on this hand that appeared for her, as if by magic. "The boy I wanted to bring back to the States with me." She struggles to find her voice to continue but turns the page instead.

The next pages show Khalil in his everyday activities—doing chores, reading a book, hugging another child, playing ball. There is one picture of herself and Khalil. They cling together, looking at the camera lens, holding on as though the slightest wind might tear them apart. Dianna crouches beside him, her hand in his wild hair. Khalil's tiny, elegant hands grasp a rock in one hand, a pencil in another.

"Where is the boy now?" Qasim asks, his voice like a gentle, prodding breeze, but all it does is stir angry fury. She doesn't want to talk about it because it'll open up the loss of Khalil, of her mother, of all these years without Qasim.

"How should I know?" The tears begin to flow, and she falls into his arms, and the tears come and come, and time stops for a while. "He's supposed to be with his mother in London," she says, finally wiping the tears away.

"He thought of you like a mother, didn't he, Dianna?" Qasim whispers into her hair. He smooths it back from her forehead and gives her eyebrows tiny kisses. She counts them. She stops at twelve, one for every year since they met.

"He's *with* his mother," she says.

"Sudan is no place for a child, but having left a son behind, given him up, so to speak, I know that a son should have two parents. He needs his father, too."

"What if his mother sends him back there? His father is far from parental, and I couldn't save him," she groans. "I couldn't do anything. Now all I can do is cry." When she can finally stop the tears from falling, she pushes away from him. His jacket is soaked through, and mascara has soaked through his lapel.

"I'm sorry," she murmurs.

"For what?"

"I've ruined your jacket. I've never wept in front of you like that. I don't cry much at all, in fact."

"You needed to."

She dabs at her eyes, trying to gain control of the grief taking hold. Tears do not help her raw emotion, this kind of deep connection. And shame that she still misses him, even though he is safe in Europe with a mother who loves him. She has no right to miss him, let alone worry about him.

"Sweetie," he continues, "I was going to wait until after dinner, but I have something for you." He reaches and fumbles around in his trouser pocket. "Where did it go now?"

Dianna gets up and goes to the bathroom mirror, wipes the mascara from underneath her eyes, blows her nose, returns to wipe her make-up off his pressed shirt. When she returns, he is holding a small silver cardboard box with a royal blue ribbon curled around it several times.

"This is for you."

Dianna's gasp holds years of yearning and worry and surprise and, finally, gratitude.

"You should have had this a long time ago. You would have if . . ." his voice trails off. His hands, clasped tight around the tiny gift box, fall toward the floor, still holding it. They are shaking.

She takes the box from him and sets it on the table. "I like to wait for my gifts," she teases. She also wants to feel calm when she opens it, to be in the moment together. "I made you dinner. Let's eat."

Dianna used to take an entire Christmas Day to open all her gifts. The anticipation is the best part of gifts for her. Now though, she is delighted and apprehensive all at once. She wants to savor the moment but fears all that's inside is an ounce of sand or a piece of cloth. Another postcard with palms that says nothing.

"You needed that," he says again about her crying jag. "I can tell you're feeling better."

She isn't, but she smiles anyway. He wants her happiness, and she wants to give it to him. "And you?" she asks. "What about you? How are you?"

"We'll touch on my news after we eat. I'm hungry!"

She takes him by the hand and leads him to the table, pulls the chair out for him, seats him, rubs his shoulders, which are as tense as a small mountain ridge.

Then she brings dinner in from the kitchen, humming something she can't recollect the name of.

"Sing for me," he says as she serves his plate. "That is beautiful." He still says the word like a breath from the Orient.

She laughs. "I've forgotten even what it is, let alone the words."

He takes her hand. "Thank you for this night, Dianna." His voice is urgent, pleading. "Sing something you know then." His grip gets tighter. "For me."

"Okay." She hasn't sung for years, not since she left the States. The only song beating through her is "Over the Rainbow." She can hear her voice, resonant and strong, echoing across to the opposite wall. Qasim closes his eyes after the first few bars.

When she finishes, all is still. She thinks he may have fallen asleep.

"Qasim?" she whispers.

"That was like a fairy song," he says, his eyes still shut. "I don't want to come back."

"But you must." She laughs. "I don't cook often, and when I do, I expect it to be eaten."

He picks up his napkin, places it in his collar, takes off his suit jacket, and rolls up his shirt sleeves.

She watches him as he eats. He holds himself back, mindful of each bite, his elegance apparent even as he swallows. She tries to compare him to the men she has known since him and finds she cannot. When she brings him dessert, brownies with specialty French vanilla ice cream on top, she kneels and kisses him, long and deep and true. Her shoulders ache; it feels so right.

He gets up, upsetting the plates on the table, and she notices, but she does not laugh this time. Only for a split second, she wishes he were larger and she smaller, so he could pick her up like a child and carry her to her bed. But then the thought leaves. He is who he is, she is who she is, and it is perfect.

She has been careful about her bed. The sheets smell of Carolina jasmine, and she has purchased new pillows. She reaches for the lamp, but he pulls her hand away. "Leave the light on. Sing for me."

He moves his hand across her body, and spasms flow down the length of it. "Slow," she whispers in his ear. She runs her fingertip over his earlobe. "Slow." And then she shows him how, singing, humming, singing again. The rhythm takes over, claims her, and after, lulls her to sleep.

When she wakes, he is not beside her, and the clock shows 2:00 a.m. She jolts up, afraid he is gone, but he is sitting in the rocker from her Gran's porch, the one she painted blue to match her room. He's watching her. He has put his trousers back on, but not his shirt. She stares at his chest, trying to etch every detail into memory. When he sees she is awake, he gets up and picks up the first box he gave her so long ago. It sits, a bit worse for having been all over the world, in the middle of her dresser. Its sheen still reflects in the mirror. "You still have this."

"Of course."

"I still have your letters and your poem."

She thinks she may weep again, but she doesn't. How could he have her letters and yet never respond to her last one? To send her mother letters instead of her? She decides not to pursue this question with him now. Instead, she moves toward him and caresses the box after him, puts his finger up to her lips, kisses it, puts it back on the box.

"I saw the lining was ripped." His voice shakes a bit.

"Yes."

"How did that happen?" He is trying to sound nonchalant.

"They tore my belongings apart in Sudan."

"Oh," he answers. She can hear the disappointment in his voice.

"Qasim, my dear, dear Qasim," she says. "I found it."

"You did?" He looks genuinely happy like when she greeted him this evening, yet more relaxed, at peace.

"Come." He pulls her toward the living room.

She pulls her robe out of her closet, throws it over her shoulders before she follows him.

"Do you remember that day?" Qasim asks as they sit side by side on the couch.

"The day we met? Or the day you gave me the Damascene mosaic box?"

"The morning after we met," he says. "I have this memory, you see, which is unforgiving."

"You say that, but what do you remember?"

"You were sitting in my wing chair. Your left leg was tucked under you. The clock said 10:03 a.m. You had on *my* robe. The sunlight hit the long, thick hair on your left shoulder. You were so, so beautiful."

Dianna reels at this information. She remembers it now, just as he does, but she had not carried it around with her as he has. Or remembered herself as beautiful. She can't speak.

"I am sorry I could never be there for you. Don't say anything," he says when she opens her mouth to convey her forgiveness. "Open the gift."

Her eyes never leave his face as she tears at the ribbon, the curly kind. The ribbon finally pops.

"Open it," he says again, with more urgency.

She takes the lid from the box. Inside is another container.

"Do you know where this box comes from?"

He's always tested her. She's not sure he believes she speaks French. "It's ceramic, Limoges."

"Tres bien."

It is porcelain, painted a gilded gold. She picks it up and holds it to the light. It is a miniature Arabian lamp.

"Rub it," he says, but he is not laughing.

She does as he asks.

"Now open it."

Inside are two pieces of curled paper, the kind found in Chinese fortune cookies. The first one says, "Love is like playing the piano.

First, you must learn to play by the rules. Then you must forget the rules and play from the heart."

"That was in my fortune cookie the night we met," he says.

"You kept it." Her heart beats against every rib in her chest.

She unrolls the second one. It is in his handwriting. The inscription is the same as what she found in the lining of the box he gave her, the one she found her last day at Biel's camp. But this time, it is encircled with a heart. "Read it to me," she says. She listens to the cadence of his Arabic, his soft, gentle voice, and then says, "Read it again."

After he repeats the sentence several times, she puts her head on his chest, feels it beat in her ear. "Which kind of love does it say you have?" she asks.

"The kind that nests in the chambers of the heart," he says. "But you know, sweetie, that is not the only word I have held in my heart when I have thought of you and our short time together. A short time that will last forever."

"I have a kind of love for you, too," she says, "though there is no word for it in English."

"Such a limited language," he teases, then grows serious. "And that word would be?"

"I have carried you with me no matter where I have been. I can't lose you. I haven't really understood it. I don't share it with anyone else because they wouldn't understand. They would think I was crazy. Sometimes I think I am crazy. At first, I thought it was just that I needed to hold onto my memories, to emulate you. But that's not all of it. Not at all."

"That would be *hayam*. Love that wanders the earth."

"*Hayam*," she repeats.

"Or perhaps *gharam*. That is what we both must have."

She kisses his eyelashes. "And that is?"

"Love that is willing to pay the price."

CHAPTER TWENTY-FOUR: LIKE OLD TIMES

August 1, 1993
New York City

She thinks about it for the month they spend together. He's given her the gift. Dare she hope she has his heart, too? Her heart says yes.

They're seeing each other most every night, but he's staying at Tariq's, for propriety's sake. So different than their time together before. This time with him seems like a dream, not grounded in reality like their relationship in the 1980s. Yet she discerns that this sort of distance is what is real in his culture. She despises giving him up to the dark night air, often in the wee hours, as he walks down the dew-covered sidewalk. Leaving both of them separated but her completely alone.

There's also the matter of her career. She's been offered the Addis job. It's taken her years, not months, to get this offer. It's tough not to accept it, but she doubts she can have Africa and Qasim, too. Yet if she turns it down, it may mean the U.N. never relinquishes another to her. She's American. She doesn't speak many languages. She doesn't have a Ph.D. And, she's a woman.

Does she fit best on her original side of the ocean, or would she be better off on his? Perhaps he wants her go-ahead to carry the relationship any farther. Perhaps he's just enjoying the moment because he feels it's best if they focus on giving back to the world instead of themselves. Theirs has never been a conventional relationship.

She's translating and editing at her rickety table when he shows up to help her look for furniture. It's a good sign, though it's quite the picture having him shop with her for anything.

He's meticulous in his research. He takes her to the best furniture store in the city, and then he examines the living room furniture as if it were a fragile treasure.

"Trash," he says a few times. She's never cared about furniture. Amusing how much he does. But then, his home had been so well decorated when they'd met, she'd suspected a woman had done it. Now she realizes he's bought the furniture, except for the family rugs. Now, if he gave her a rug, she'd know he was proposing!

"That one is fine," she says, plopping down on a sofa, spent. "The coffee table goes with it. Let's just get it and go."

He scowls. "This furniture is improperly constructed. There's no dovetailing. It's pasted together."

She has no idea what he means until he shows her. "Dovetailing used to be the norm," he explains.

They finally find a dovetailed chest, a round dining table, and a coffee table that meets his high expectations. They leave without a sofa, which is what she really needs. They'll deliver it tomorrow. He's whistling as he holds the door open for her.

She's happy he's in a good mood. He's seemed far away the past few days, complaining about Tariq and his new girlfriend, his profession. She's learned not to encroach on his parental territory.

"Now I can throw a dinner party," she says.

His brow goes up.

"Not an embassy party," she teases. "I know you despise those. A friends-and-family party."

"Your brother and sister?" His voice sounds shocked.

"No, they can't afford to come."

"Of course, they can, Dianna. It's just a drive."

"They won't come, then."

"What about your family members?" she asks.

"I have no family members here, other than Tariq. Or real friends . . . even Jamal . . ."

She cuts him off at the mention of that despicable man's name. "No, just people we both know. Tariq. His girlfriend, Laila. He can invite others if he wants. My friends from Southern Sudan. Leah, Sophia, you know."

By now, they're inside her apartment. He pulls her close, and she can smell his skin. He's not used cologne today at her request. His skin smells like something out of this world, but something of her world. Where they join.

She starts to kiss his neck but then notices his serious expression. "What's wrong?"

"Are you not heading to Addis, then, Dianna?"

She hedges. "Why would I let you purchase furniture for me if I was leaving New York? You know about the conflict between my department and the Ethiopian delegation," she says. She's waffling.

"That has gone on for too long."

"I know. And it's finally come to resolution." She tries to find the right words. She doesn't want him to think she's going to decline it for him.

"You need to know I will never stand in the way of your career, sweetie. I never tried to. You thought a few times I was. But I was trying to protect you. It was a different time. Men were . . . men."

"And never the twain would meet except in the bedroom?" She couldn't suppress a smirk.

"Something like that. I am sorry. I did not make those rules."

"You seemed to abide by them."

"Dianna, I was in love with you. How could I not?"

"And I with you."

"You make it seem wrong."

"I thought you might see it as wrong."

"How can love, expressed, ever be wrong?"

"I agree."

"Well, that's settled then." He gets up and pours himself a Scotch from the decanter she's put it in for his benefit. The afternoon light glints off it.

"Please come back," she whispers.

He returns and nuzzles her neck, kisses her hair.

"Before we go any further . . ." She's jerking him around not answering his question. Now she's gone and done it.

He backs up, takes a swig of Scotch, and frowns. "Hold on," she says. "It's simple enough what I have to say. If I refuse the Addis job, it won't be because of you, or even us. I'm not certain there is an us yet."

"There has always been an 'us.'"

"No, I don't mean that. I mean, isn't there a middle road? Where we can have our careers and one another, too?" There, she's stated what she wants. Love and a career. Other women have both. Why can't she?

He moves away this time, almost to the other side of the couch. The silence penetrates her heart more than his distance.

"Dianna, dearest, there's something I must take care of back home."

"For how long?"

"To take care of this . . . family matter . . . I must take a mission."

"For how long?"

"At least six months."

She gets up and paces the room. She's more confused than angry. "When were you going to tell me?"

"Today."

"At the furniture store?" Was that a bribe to calm her before taking his leave?

"No, of course not. After . . ."

She understands his need to delay any truth-telling. This month has been idyllic. The Cinderella slipper before she goes "Into the Woods." But there are always woods in life, whether you go it alone or with someone you love.

"Tell me." She's using his words, those familiar words.

He smiles in recognition, too. "It's something I need to do before I explain it."

"Very well, Qasim. I must have faith in you, then."

He looks down at the floor. "Thank you."

Is he ashamed? "Please be worthy of my trust."

"I will, my darling. I will return with news."

She wants to wrap herself around him. She can tell he wants the same thing. Instead, she speaks words she should have said long ago. "Each time we lose touch, I'm resigned to my fate, Qasim. Yet I'm lonely. Please don't leave me lonely for long."

"Do you think I am not lonely as well?"

"This time is different for me, somehow. I know, I truly know, I will see you again, though not where or how."

"It need not be that mysterious. I've always known we would meet again. Hoped we would be together."

"I knew it, too. Always thought it might be in Heaven."

"My God. I hope it's long before then."

"It's up to you. I'm here for you, in New York, Beirut, Nairobi, Addis. Name your place."

"Then it won't be long." He sweeps her into his arms. They don't have long now. The clock ticks out its eternal knell as they make love.

When they bid each other farewell, she asks him when he will depart for the Middle East.

"Next week."

She'd known he'd already decided to leave long before he spoke of it. Her heart sinks despite the truth he's told her. It's only part of the truth. "So long, then," is all she says.

CHAPTER TWENTY-FIVE: WOUNDS

November 1, 1993
New York City

When her job in Addis was offered, she asked for a pay increase, and they refused it, just as she thought they would. She turned it down. It may have been her own self-sabotage, but maybe it was that she wanted to make a final decision. She heard through the U.N. grapevine that the job had gone to a new employee, a young male rising star who recently got his masters in African Studies.

She continues to translate and toys with finishing another degree. She hosts get-togethers for her diminishing circle of single friends who congregate around her beautiful new furniture. She thinks of changing apartments but then decides to stay put. She won't let herself believe it is because she wants Qasim to be able to find her. Her chest tightens when she thinks of him.

People are carrying phones these days, but she's lucky enough not to have one yet, to be at the Under-Secretary General's beck and call. Yet, at least Qasim could find her in the U.S. if she had one. It won't be long before the phone's not her decision anyway.

He's sent a postcard with

"Thinking of you. Sending my warmest regards. Love, Qasim"

No mention of news or date of departure. At least it wasn't a picture of a hotel pool, which is what he used to send. It was of Beirut's seaside, the Corniche. Now she wonders where he is, if he's thinking of her, when he'll return. She won't fool herself it will ever be "for good." It was one thing when his arms were around her, professing love, sharing her love. Another sitting here alone. These days she has animal babies to give her a little love.

Leah adopted two cats from the pound, and Dianna's babysitting them for her while she's on a prolonged business trip. Dianna confuses their names, so she calls them Thing One and Thing Two. They've developed a sort of feline basketball game. She's got one trash bin labeled "Dispensable," the other labeled "Indispensable." She's discovered one reason she hadn't been chosen for a mission before was that her boss in Translations labeled Dianna as "indispensable" to his department.

"Score!" Dianna shouts each time she makes a basket without either Thing One or Two intercepting her paper wad. Thing One looks baffled, and Thing Two hides behind the curtains, his tail bushed. There, she's frightened them, and they are her only audience. She yawns. It's late. She feeds Thing One dried and Thing Two canned. Then heads to bed without her own dinner.

She gets the call in the middle of the night. At first, she thinks Qasim's voice is a dream, that she is still sleeping.

"Dianna?"

"Where are you?" She pushes herself up on her pillows, disturbing the cats. Thing Two comes and nudges his head into her hand, asking if it is morning yet. Thing One gives her a look of contempt.

"I'm here, in New York."

"What?" He's only been gone four months. He'd said six, and she'd expected longer.

She fumbles for the lamp switch on her bedside table. When she flicks it, light floods the room, and everyone squints. Thing One is totally disgusted now. He jumps down and crawls under the bed. Thing Two kneads the coverlet and mews.

"How long will you be here?" She's as annoyed as the cats. Why is he calling in the middle of the night?

"Not for long."

"Why did you call?" She hears the exasperation in her tone.

"I wanted to hear your voice."

She notices his voice is gravelly with a rushed breathiness. "Are you alright?" she asks. Her heart starts beating harder against her ribs. He's not due back to the States yet.

"Yes. Yes, of course."

Silence. The clock ticks in the background. She doesn't know what to say now. Why would he be calling at 2:00 a.m. if he was alright?

"Can I see you?" Qasim asks finally. His breath is becoming labored. That's strange. Is he anxious calling her?

"When?" He should know better than to call her in the middle of the night asking to see her at the last minute. "Well, actually, I have a couple of presentations to make tomorrow." Dianna fusses with the covers. Thing One snatches a corner with his claws, still underneath the box spring. Silence.

"I could meet you for coffee in between."

More silence. There's definitely something wrong.

"What's the matter, Qasim?" She opens the curtains to glance outside, partially expecting him to be standing there for her to buzz him in. Not a single person is within view.

"There's nothing the matter."

"There is." She's pacing back and forth now, and the cats think she's playing. They hide and pounce each time she passes the bed.

"Well, they just have to do a few tests on my heart and kidneys."

"I can see you afterward." She sits back down on the bed, picking at the covers. If the U.N. sent him back to the U.S. instead of finding him treatment in-country, his health, if not his life, is in danger. Has he been attacked? Shot? Then she remembers the last time he had kidney problems.

"That may not be possible. I'm in the hospital. I was going to ask you to come have coffee with me here." The last time he'd been gravely ill, he hadn't called her. Now he's inviting her in. She tries to piece together her feelings. He's called her, which means he thinks they're in a serious relationship, yet if he's called her, it could be to say goodbye. It's always more serious than he lets on.

Something bangs against her window and makes her jump, and she stifles a scream. She rushes to the window. Looks out. A murder of squawking crows flies into the night air. Did that mean death or good fortune? She can't remember.

"Am I that scary?" he asks. She can tell he's stifling laughter because he's in pain. She leaps up and starts to dress.

"The wind is picking up," she replies. It's blustery tonight. "The city had flurries yesterday. We're in for a long winter."

"Wind?" Qasim is asking.

"You probably can't hear it if you're in a big building."

"Yes, well . . ."

"Qasim, I'm coming to see you. Where are you?"

Silence.

"Qasim?" She stumbles against her chest of drawers, and a make-up case full of cosmetics comes crashing to the floor, shattering something inside.

"Dianna. Don't come. I just needed to hear your voice."

That last night he told her not to come more than a decade ago. Kidney stones were supposed to be the worst pain there was. She'd thought he had a girlfriend, a girl other than herself, there, caring for him. She paces and swallows the panic down. *What if he is dying?*

"Dianna, just say . . . just say goodbye." His voice trails off, and that makes her sad and frightened at the same time.

"No."

Silence.

"Qasim?"

"Columbia Presbyterian. Room 1542. Can you come tonight?"

"Of course."

She places the phone down, dashes for her closet, and pulls out the first clothes she sees.

The wind is really picking up now. It's banging the garbage receptacles outside. She pulls a sweatshirt on, and it catches on her watch. She tries to free the watch and sticks her finger in her eye.

"Damn it to hell!" she screams, and the cats scatter. She takes the stairs two at a time and flags a taxi. The wind is everywhere, sending her hair into her face, blowing debris up her coat.

"Where to, Lady?"

"Columbia Presbyterian."

"Know the best way?" The cabbie is chewing—maybe his dinner, maybe gum, perhaps even tobacco. The cab reeks of it.

"How would I know?"

"You live here, don't you?"

"You don't?" Cab drivers are supposed to deliver babies sometimes, and this one doesn't even know how to find the hospital in an emergency.

"As a matter of fact, I live in Jersey City. Ever been to Jersey City?" The man sneers over the seat.

"Can you just be quiet and figure out where we're going?" Dianna crosses her arms over her chest. She's got to hurry. What if Qasim gets up and leaves before she can get there?

The last time she felt dread like this was when Driver drove her back to camp more than two years ago. Desperation so strong you couldn't weep, had no way of releasing.

What if he's not alone? She must compose herself.

"Sure." The cabbie shrugs and radios in, asking for directions. He pushes buttons on his machine in front, fixing his route. He looks in his rearview mirror at her. "That good enough for you?"

"Fine." Dianna bundles herself against the increasing cold. What happened to this taxi's heater?

"Supposed to snow tomorrow."

"I wouldn't know." Driver would have her there by now.

"Hey, Lady, what's up with you?"

"Just shut the hell up!" That silences him.

They zip past the theatres, lined up and glowing even at this late hour, then make an abrupt turn as the hospital rises before them. It looks a bit like the witch's castle in the Wizard of Oz, which reminds her of that song she sang him. Something sweet amid her menacing thoughts.

She slips past the nurses' desk. The odors of the hospital assault her, just as they always do. She tries to rid her mind of her mother's hospital stay, of field hospitals she's visited all over Africa. Her stomach churns as she slips into Qasim's room. Some of the smells are coming from it. He must be really sick.

He is sitting up in bed and flipping through a pile of documents. It's 4:00 a.m., and it's obvious he hasn't slept, even with hospital meds. He closes the briefcase by his side when she enters. "Hi, sweetie," he says, as though he just saw her yesterday.

She looks down at a bag beneath his bed filled with urine with a pinkish tinge—blood. "Oh my God," she says. Her heart races. If she could, she'd let him have some of its beats.

"I'll be fine." His eyebrows rise and fall, and he tries to smile.

"Are you in pain?"

"Not much. The drugs are really good here. Best place to go for drugs." He laughs in earnest now. "I'd trade them all for a stiff Scotch."

She goes to take his hand, but she can't. It's infested with tubing and adhesive. His elegant fingers are puffy, and his hand is black and blue. "Can I get you something?"

"No, I'm fasting until tomorrow morning. They told me I need a procedure."

She walks around and grasps his other hand and kisses it. "What's wrong?" She brings in serenity. She can't add to his burden with her panic. His blanched face makes her wonder if he'll survive the surgery.

"Just had a little angina," he says. "I've had it for a while. They're just going to check for blockage."

"But your kidneys?"

"My kidneys. My kidneys. They've always been a problem. They'll be fine. Don't worry. Just talk about how you are, what you're doing."

She stands there, wondering whether to obey.

"Go on."

"I'm caring for two cats."

"Such a poor substitution for Africa."

"An abysmal substitution for you."

"Dianna!" he scolds. "Don't say that!" But his eyes are laughing. "What are you translating?"

She doesn't answer.

"How's the U.N.?"

Is he trying to get his mind off his pain? Or is he trying to dodge her questions? She wants to ask where he's been, but she also wants to keep him relaxed. She came to support him, not interrogate him.

"It's okay. I didn't get the Addis job." She doesn't tell him she didn't want it as much as a life with him.

"Oh no! I thought . . ."

"It's fine. I finally decided I couldn't single-handedly change the world."

"They don't value you enough." He shifts his legs and grimaces.

"How was *your* mission?" she asks him.

"Just a little diplomatic paper pushing."

"How little changes in your life." She gives him a smirk.

"I could say the same about you these days." His eyes light up. "You know they are promoting me again. I think I'll take this position, but then I'll consider retirement."

"But you're back here?"

"Yes, but I think they'll send me to Beirut now. And if they do, that's where I'll stay."

Now's not the time to talk about a future together. "You'll have to let me know if one can go home again," she says and strokes his face. It is clammy, almost cold.

"I will," he says and laughs, then chokes. He looks as if he might continue but can't. Finally, he gets out: "You might see for yourself."

A nurse appears in the doorway and stares at them both. "You okay?" she asks Qasim, and when he nods, she says, "She'd better be gone in five minutes. You're supposed to rest."

"I can stay in the lobby until you go in for the tests," she says. She touches his cheek, just like the last time she touched it. They shouldn't be here again, so close and unable to admit they are together. History dealing out another ironic hand. They move toward each other, only to have something come in and block them again. "I can stay," she says again.

"No, I think not."

"Am I tiring you?"

He looks down at the wires that snake around his bed. "No . . .

Yes. I mean, you have to work tomorrow." He won't look her in the eyes.

"Are you sure you'll be alright?" she asks. Is his remoteness from the drugs being pumped into him, because he thinks he's dying, or something, or someone, else?

"Of course." His breathing gives him away. He's in pain.

"You'll call me to let me know how you are?"

"Of course."

"How long will you be here?"

"I'll go back when they decide what's wrong, but I'll see you as soon as they spring me from here."

"What if you need major surgery?"

"I won't need more surgery."

"But what if you do?"

"Then I'll have surgery."

"I'll be here."

"Dianna," he hesitates, gulps for air. "There is something you should know."

She suspects what he is going to say. It's a deathbed confession. He is married, after all. He never divorced his first wife. Why hadn't Tariq mentioned it?

At least she will finally know.

"Go get my wallet out of the trousers in the armoire," he says.

Dianna does as she is told. She plunges her hand into his pockets. The first one is completely empty. The second one yields a thick, stylish pen, an herbal tea bag, and his wallet—black Italian leather.

"Open it," he says. "Look in the credit card section."

Dianna pulls out an American Express card, a AAA card with Tariq's name on it, probably because Tariq's an American resident, a card with a gold seal and Arabic on it, and a plastic photo case. She recognizes Tariq's image immediately, although he looks fuller through his face.

"Bring it to me," Qasim says, and he winces.

"Are you in pain?" Dianna asks.

"Of a sort," he replies.

Dianna remains standing by the locker and flips through the photographs. There is a much younger Qasim, getting a diploma. "When was this taken?" She holds the photo up for him to see.

"That was right before I met you," he says, squinting. "I was getting my Ph.D. Bring it over here, Dianna."

Dianna flips to the next photo. This time she sees Qasim with the rest of his family: a tiny mother with hair down her back, a stern father with graying temples, three boys who seem to be teasing each other into laughing for the camera, and a beautiful young girl, who appears to be in between the eldest and the middle brother in age. Qasim kneels in front, the baby, maybe eighteen months, at the edge of the family, giggling.

"I always wondered what your siblings looked like. And there's your sister who died."

"Yes, you remember she died when I was still young."

"I know," Dianna says.

"Come here, Dianna," he says. "I made Tariq return home to pick up some of my belongings. I sent him away because he was arguing with both me and the medical staff, and I hope he won't return till morning. But . . . you never know."

She finally obeys because she can't stand the pain in his voice. It touches her heart even though she doesn't want to know what will happen next.

She hands the photo case to him. "Go ahead," she says. "I already know what you're going to show me."

"Dianna, I am not married," he says in a steady voice. "I wasn't in the 80s, and I am certainly not now."

Her eyes sting despite her preparation. "I knew it," she says before she has heard his words. How like him to come forth with this admission when he knows she will control her anger. It sizzles through her veins like strong bleach. Then she truly hears what he's said. "Not married?"

He turns the photos over to the very last fold. "It's not what you think," he says. He reaches over to her with his right hand and grimaces again. "Please, come here. This is difficult, if not impossible, for me to tell you." Tears trail down his cheeks. She's never seen him cry. How medicated is he? She walks toward him, then stands stiff, expectant. The wind whistles outside like a chorus.

He shows her the image, and she grimaces. Yet the face is different than what she expected. This is not the same woman in the wedding album he had shown her a decade ago. It is another young woman, only a bit older than herself. She has long auburn hair, a crooked nose, and large eyes with eyelashes that go on and on.

"This is Larissa," he explains. "I met her in Bosnia while you and I were apart. We were both lonely, and it was time . . . to move on. I didn't ever think you would consider coming back to me. I didn't even know where you were. She is a good woman. If I had only known . . ."

Tears fall in a torrent and drip onto the sheet. They trickle down the tubing. He wipes them with his free hand. ". . . that I would see you again." His voice catches, and the choking begins in earnest. "That you would have me. I went to tell her. I was going to tell her . . ."

Dianna sits down on the linoleum floor. She wants to know what she is feeling, but she can't find it. It's as though she has been given an I.V. herself. Why is he telling her this now, to absolve himself? How can she openly react at all now, with him ill?

"Dianna?" Qasim queries. "Dianna?"

"You love her?" Dianna finally asks.

"Of a sort."

"She is Muslim?"

"Her father was, but she wasn't raised in any particular faith."

"Oh." Dianna sits there for a while, listening to the monitor's steady beat. *The timing still isn't right for us*, she thinks.

Qasim seems to be reading her mind. "There's no need to analyze it, Dianna. We had what we had. She and I have what you and I have now. A lot can be said for a dear friendship."

"Ours or yours with her?"

He hesitates. "Both. I cannot imagine being with anyone I was not friends with. What she and I have, it is different than what you and I had. We were both alone, and we needed . . . companionship. I was going to tell her about you, about us, but . . . but I fell ill."

No, it was more than timing, wasn't it? She wants to scream at him. She wants to ask what kind of Arabic love he and Larissa share. But she doesn't want that to be the way he remembers her. It's not the last moments she wants to remember of him. He is so deathly pale, and he's not telling her the whole story about his health, his hospitalization. And probably not Larissa.

"Well then, we must be practical." Dianna paces her words, hiding the rip in her core that threatens to unseat her. She's beginning to perspire. She wants to run into the wind, fast enough to fly, fly away. She rises to leave.

Qasim closes his eyes. He does not want to see her pain. He has enough to bear himself.

"I was sitting here, with these tubes, and all I could think of was you. Not her. Not Tariq's mother. Not even my mother. Only you, Dianna."

She says nothing. She has never put practicality and love in the same sentence before. She never imagined Qasim uttering the words that still hang in the room, blotting out the smell of germs and disinfectant.

"And I wanted you to know that I've asked Jamal to help me find Khalil. He hasn't found him, not yet, but I have hope. I want you to see that he's fine." Qasim reaches out his free arm toward her, but she doesn't respond. She stands there, limp and leaden.

"Why is it always Jamal? First, you do his bidding. Then he does yours. And now there's yet another woman in your life. What about me?" She watches one lone tear trickle from her right eye onto the sterile tile floor, wipes it away with her shoe. "You need to decide what you want, once and for all."

"I've always wanted you. It was you who didn't want me," he says.

"What?"

"That's why I'm going back, the moment I'm well enough, to let her know that you want me."

She's dizzy, feels as if she'll faint. "We can talk about this later. You need to rest." She says these words, but her feelings are something else again. Anger boils up from a well inside she didn't know existed. Not rage. She loves him too much. But anger, disappointment, rejection that he's kept a secret from her yet again.

"You do want me, don't you?" he asks.

A skinny nurse with salt-and-pepper hair that spills in every direction enters the room with a hypodermic. Qasim grimaces. Dianna's unuttered answer hangs in the air. The nurse manipulates the tubes and sticks the needle into one. "This will sting," she advises.

"Who is this?" she asks Qasim while she looks at Dianna.

The three of them listen to the E.K.G. monitor's rhythmic beep. That is his heart, the beat of his heart. Despite her grief, her heart beats right along with his.

"She needs to leave," the nurse says.

"She's my sister." Qasim's chuckle is half remorseful, half conspiratorial.

Dianna places one hand over his chest, her other on her chest. She needs to sort her feelings out. She has no idea of her answer. How can you leave the man you love for the last time? How can you say "yes" to someone you don't completely trust? She leans over and kisses his forehead, hoping against hope she will kiss him again soon.

The nurse rolls her eyes. "And I'm your long-lost cousin," she says. "I've seen what your family looks like, and she isn't part of it. She needs to leave."

Dianna rises, retrieves her jacket, and heads for the door. She turns in the hallway and looks back at him.

"I will call you as soon as I'm out," Qasim says.

She doesn't answer. She just stares at him. He'll have family here tomorrow, and she's not part of it. She knows how serious his illness is, and so does he. She wants to remember every detail, the way he does her. She looks up at the clock. It's 5:00 a.m. Another day.

"Say goodbye, Dianna," he says and turns away from her.

"Goodbye, Qasim," Dianna says.

"I will call you," Qasim calls down the hall.

CHAPTER TWENTY-SIX: ACCORD

The Next Day
New York City

Dianna calls the hospital at lunchtime. The I.C.U. nurse tells her that Qasim is in surgery and that she cannot tell her anything else because Dianna is not his next of kin. She knows better than to go wait for him to be out. She tries Tariq, but his phone goes to voicemail. Her heart breaks at Tariq's voice, which resonates like his dad's. She has no such recording of Qasim's voice. She wonders if he'll even speak to her again if . . . No, she won't think of death. Not now.

She calls the hospital again that night, and another nurse tells her Qasim is out of surgery. Dianna finally wheedles a little information out of this one. He is stable.

She'll visit in the morning. It would upset him to come now. She fantasizes instead. About being together. What would it be like to marry him? Part like coming home at last. Part like leaving home forever. But wasn't leaving home part of being an adult? The Dianna that was lost is now found.

She falls asleep trying to craft what she'll say, not knowing what she'll say. She dreams.

She's taking a shower when he arrives home. Throws on his robe. Wraps a towel around her head.

"You aren't ready to go?" Qasim asks with a raised brow. She tells him no, and he says he'll have to go on ahead of her.

She's laid out her clothes on the bed, an evening suit with a long jacket, royal blue in color. She feels the nubby silk and feels a box hiding beneath them. She pulls the box out, a royal blue velvet box that practically matches her outfit with silver writing inscribed across it: "Baldwin, Browning, and Billings," a designer she's always coveted. She opens the box to find a strand of pearls and pearl-and-aquamarine drop earrings to match nestled within. "To match your eyes," the card reads.

She hurries to catch up, but he's waiting for her. She grins, but only for a moment. Then she remembers.

He's never waited for her. Qasim does not wait for anyone.

She wakes up before the alarm, full of insight only dreams can offer. She hasn't waited for him either. She's a runner, just like he is. No matter what's to come, she doesn't want to run anymore.

● ● ●

He's in a twilight sleep when she arrives at the hospital, but he stirs and smiles at her. Tariq gives her a kiss on both cheeks.

"He's going to pull through," he whispers. "He needs his rest, though."

"No small feat for him," she says.

"Some family and friends arrive in an hour. Some have flown for hours. I'm sure he wants some quiet time with you beforehand."

"Now's not the time for me to be here and cause him stress. I'll only stay a few minutes."

"Thank you, Dianna. I'll leave you two alone for now." Tariq slips out of the room.

She clasps his hand. She puts her head down and dozes with him, traveling again to that place where they can be in love, happy, together. It is a place with no time. When she stirs, it's been forty-five minutes. Tariq is nowhere to be found. She checks with the nurse, who checks Qasim's vitals, saying he's doing well. She's due back at work. She thinks of leaving him a note. She returns to his room and perches on the window, trying to find words. Cannot. She watches his troubled slumber, full of beeps and tubes. And then she leaves. For now.

● ● ● ● ●

She can't go to work. Qasim, now, he would have gone to work, but her mind races. Not enough translating words can quiet it. Instead, she wanders Manhattan. She winds up on the big stone steps flanked by lions outside the New York Public Library. Better to make this decision alone than ask a friend's opinion. Even Sophia's. They are living their own lives, wield their own opinions.

Her musings take her to childhood, sequestered in the musty stacks of her town's library, reading books on archaeology. Pushing her sister and brother in a wheelbarrow. Leaping into the color of fallen leaves. A Cracker Jack prize she retrieved when she was a girl. It was a tiny yet loaded futuristic book showing inventions of the 21st century. She had counted on her fingers how old she'd be in the year 2000 . . . 40, 41, 42, 43.

She could almost imagine being as old as her parents. She'd never imagined being alone. It has happened despite her suspended disbelief. She takes out a notepad and lists her blessings: friends, a modicum of success helping others, food on the table, lack of malaria. Then she draws a vertical line and writes down her dreams: travel, adventure, exhilaration, freedom. In the middle, she puts a circle with Qasim inside it. She puts pen to mouth as she ponders whether she should write down "love." It strikes her that she has it without the strings of matrimony. She shifts on the hard steps, wondering what if. She shakes her head from side to side and decides not to write "L-O-V-E" down. She's had it with too many complications.

What would she change then? She grins—who will see this list anyway—and returns to her balance sheet and writes "EMPOWERMENT" in capital letters.

She doesn't mean the power a C.E.O. exerts over his employees' lives or the power a tycoon shows off at his club. Nor does she mean the self-interested, corrupt power she has seen time and again in international leaders. She would like the power to change things just a bit, even in her own life. She will never be completely fulfilled living in an apartment with two good friends a few flights down, even if she is a sort of foster mom to Leah's cats. Comfortable, yes, but not happy.

Did love bring happiness? Did it bring power? Didn't Solomon's Biblical love song say that love was as strong as death? Now that was power.

Her mind drifts to her dates that had led nowhere: superficial relationships without that power, without that love, the come up "for a drink" hints, the same litany of conversation. She has not met a man in years who can speak of subjects beyond his last work assignment, meal, or golf swing.

She stares down at her sheet of checks and balances. She realizes with a start that she might be fooling herself. Maybe in this lifetime, there was only one man. Her first love Danson was simply a prelude to the main feature, over before the reel ended. Up until now, she chose not to believe this. She jerks herself upright. Wow, she's around Qasim's age when they first met.

The breeze picks up. She winds her way home. She goes to the bathroom mirror and gazes at her lines. Who invented mirrors anyway? Before the mirror, your beauty was mirrored back at you by other people, not some oversized piece of glass, or yourself. As she pats at the lines that make her brow a permanent furrow, she decides that something must change.

The phone ring jolts her. His voice tells her he's okay.

"Dianna?" Qasim sounds as if he thinks she has left for good. She can hear the confusion of the medications, but she also hears something uncommon for him, a tone between pathos and panic.

"How are you?" she asks. "I'm here. I'm coming back right now."

CHAPTER TWENTY-SEVEN: SO LONG

February 1, 1994
New York City

"I must leave again, Dianna," Qasim says. It's been three short months, and he's been staying at Tariq's.

"Already?" He'd been too weak to go out for New Year's Eve, which made it special. The first week, they'd not even kissed. She simply brought him gifts from the outside world, told him stories about her day. She'd walk in, and he'd immediately say, "Tell me." Like old times. Except it wasn't old times.

Gradually, they succumbed to kissing, but she was thinking of separating once he got fully back on his feet. She didn't want that woman Larissa to feel like she did in the early 80s. She didn't want to feel like she had in that hospital, a third wheel, again.

The New Year's holiday had changed her mind. And now he was leaving, and she still didn't know the final answer to the question he asked her in the hospital. She hates her vacillation between "yes" and "no." Her heart beats against her stomach, half desire, half fear.

"Just for a few weeks. We need to speak before I go."

"I'm all ears."

"I think it's your turn to speak." He's referring to the night before his surgery when the nurse interrupted.

"You are with another woman. It seems to be always the case."

"Dianna, Larissa and I are not married. She and I never were going to marry. We stopped any romance a couple of years ago. It wasn't working."

His gaze tells her that may not have been true before his recent hospital visit. Even so, Larissa's not here by his side. "For you or Larissa? Maybe we should just remain . . ."

She searches for a word to describe them other than that word he said, meaning "love willing to pay the price."

"But what do you want? You didn't want me then. You're great at telling me what I want, though you're often incorrect. What do you want *now, really?*" He's propped on her couch, and he struggles to sit upright.

She reaches to steady him. "No, stay put, Qasim. I have been giving it thought. You just come out of nowhere asking me what I want when you're attached, and I have no idea what you want."

"*Was* attached. Isn't it obvious? And I haven't 'come out of nowhere' since Nairobi." His hands reach to the heavens, then he winces. "Dianna, don't run away from me, not this time."

"No. It's not obvious. Not to me."

"I . . ." His eyes dart around the room as they used to. She hasn't seen his caged animal look in a decade. "Dianna, I want us to be a family if we can. In whatever form you'd like. Dianna, I want you."

She wants to lean into him and ask him to hold her forever. Instead, she says, "Give me time to think about it while you're away. If you can't tie up your loose ends with her—or anyone else—it's not about me. You can't leave her for me. You need to leave her because you want to, with or without me. I'll have my answer when you call me."

"I've already left her. I just need to make sure she understands. Like you did with me."

"You didn't seem to understand I'd left."

"And neither does she." Qasim looks her straight in the eye. "We both have learned we have to put all our cards on the table. No room for miscommunication. And I must do it in person. You didn't do that for me."

"But I did. I also sent the letter."

"What letter?" His confusion seems genuine.

"The letter I sent you," she says.

"When?"

She reaches in her heart for the date, retrieves it: "April 10, 1983."

"I never received such a letter."

"But you must have." She walks to the window. "You really didn't, then?"

"No. What did it say?"

She laughs. "I gave you back to family, country, and Jamal."

"Never. I repeat N-E-V-E-R." The other time he spelled out a word, it was in English: "D-I-V-O-R-C-E-D."

He's telling the truth. "I'm sorry I didn't believe you."

When she looks up because he does not answer, his eyes are full of tears. His gaze penetrates her. It's the moment she's always dreamed of, and yet, he's right. She does feel like running away. She's been running ever since she left her mother, father, and siblings. Maybe she ran away from Africa in a way? She's been running away from home all this time. She won't anymore.

She wipes a tear away, brings it to her mouth, and tastes its saltiness. "It's probably *yes,* Qasim."

His kiss is full of a sweetness she's never tasted before.

Chapter Twenty-eight: Contracts

February 28, 1994
New York City

Does she fit best on her original side of the ocean, or would she be better off on his? Maybe both. She translates, edits, and gets an unexpected inter-departmental promotion. She throws dinner parties. Cleans the apartment top to bottom. Travels home to see her siblings. They drive her mad, so she returns to the city.

She has too much time on her hands to think, and a month passes with no word from Qasim. She grows irritated with his silence and anxious that it will continue. Maybe he's reunited with the woman who was waiting for him overseas, just as Dianna waits here. Leah has begun to travel more. Aisha has linked in with the Southern Sudanese immigrant community. When she's not with them, she's caring for her children or in an E.S.O.L. program. Her husband may be able to enter the U.S. this year.

She decides to go check her mail and go to the park. She's recently purchased some rollerblades. She almost drops the tissue-thin letter when she finds it in her postal box. It's addressed in a fine European or Arabic writer's hand, a script so fine it reminds her of Qasim's postcards long ago. Her heart skips a double beat, but it's from Mirembe. She's settled into a job on the West Coast, but she's coming to New York for a conference. She'd like to see Dianna. Dianna turns around. She goes upstairs and writes back, extending hospitality.

She gets up in the wee hours, re-reads it, and then decides to install software on her new computer to protect it from viruses. Simulated robots that look like Pac men with stick arms and legs demonstrate how to load software. She mutters to herself as she writes down the directions. She'll have to fiddle with it once she's at work. If all goes well, she won't have to get a tech nerd to show her. They all act like everything is her fault. It's just another obstacle life has thrown in for good measure. Certain things about life here remind her of Sudan, only with more bureaucracy added in. Sudan taught her to endure it and struggle on, anticipating the next moment, trying to salvage hope. If the Sudanese could keep going, despite war, separation, famine, and death, who is she to worry?

The phone rings, and she jolts out of her cursor-induced trance. Her heart skips a beat. Worry seeps into her blood before she hears his voice. He sounds fine. It's now or never.

He's called sooner than she'd expected. Doubt seeps in again. Who is this man? Is he the Qasim who works for world peace? Is he the Qasim of a thousand secrets? The Qasim she has held to her heart? Or the Qasim who, no matter his personal beliefs, must, by way of his responsibilities, work within a system that is both corrupt and the world's only hope?

"I've missed you."

She listens to the thud against her ribs for a while before she answers him.

"Hello? Dianna?" His voice is crisp and clear. Where is he?

"How's your family?"

"Tariq is fine. My brothers are fine."

"And your ex-wife?"

"She is fine." She hears a decibel of irritation enter the otherwise static-free connection. "What's new?" he asks after a significant pause.

She can tell there is something wrong. "And your other . . . girlfriend?"

More silence. She begins to pace to and from table to kitchen, then to spoon grounds into her coffee maker. She needs to be acutely aware.

"Dianna?"

She's peeved. Thinking about being with him when he's attached to another woman disgusts her.

"I think I finally may be coming to your part of the world," she says, even though she doesn't know how she'll pull it off yet. She wants to give him an out if he needs one.

"Oh?"

"Yes, I met some official at a cocktail party who put in a good word for me."

Who knows what will happen, but it's conversation at least. Conversation that will lead to discovering how he's feeling about her. She hears that old familiar chuckle that starts in his throat and then grows higher in pitch.

"Are you laughing at me?" She bangs an overhead cabinet with the back of her hand.

"No, of course not. I was laughing at the ironies of life."

"What do you mean?"

"I'm back in New York. I've rented a place not that far from you. I'm thinking of buying a place."

So that was the reason for such a clear connection. She feels irritation that she has not heard from him but then chastens herself. She struggles to eradicate the doubt seeping back into her heart and spreading through her arteries. She used to think of herself as his "New York" girl. The pit of her stomach churns.

"Dianna, when can we meet? I have a lot to share with you about . . ." He pauses. "Us."

She feels the pounding in her chest become pronounced again. Grounds spill on the counter. "I'm not sure."

"Why?" His voice is penitent. "Are we not dear friends at the very least?"

"We've been friends with differences," Dianna says at last, with only a slight break in her voice. "I want to make sure they're mended."

"Dianna," his voice is now full of reproach. "Do you really think one can stop wanting something simply through willpower?"

She contemplates this, taking the question as sincere instead of merely manipulative. "Qasim, why are you calling me this early in the morning?"

"Because I could not sleep, thinking about seeing you."

"No," her voice comes out soft and, she is afraid, weak. "You're acting as though we're free to follow our desire. As though the freedom to do what we wish with one another ever existed. I, for one, put other people's feelings before my whims. I keep in touch with the people I care for. How can we expect to with a world between us? Every call costs a hundred dollars." She throws her free hand into the air. "Oh, hell, maybe it's just cultural difference . . ."

His laughter echoes again, and she smiles in reminiscence. "Dianna, why would you say love has anything to do with culture? You think I don't care about other people because I am Arab?"

She laughs a thin minor scale. "I see your point. I guess love and kindness, or the lack thereof, surpass culture."

"Yes," he says. "Now, would you deny me the opportunity to have a coffee with you?"

There, he's probably got bad news, or he would have shown up at her doorstep. She sits down, hearing her morning coffee whir through the container, inhaling a strong hazelnut essence. She mentally picks at the emotional scab that has formed since their last meeting. Does she dare tear it off again if he's going to stay with this other woman?

Sophia's voice comes to mind now. "The pain dulls with time." Yet it hurts more now than the first time when he'd revealed he had another life months after they had met. She checks herself. Is she running? Is her fear of emotional pain or even of societal judgment keeping her from happiness? Sophia also said, "Take advantage of each moment to be happy."

Dianna twirls an imaginary cord on her cordless phone, then begins to twirl a strand of her own hair one way, then the other. Perhaps Sophia is wrong on both counts. She still feels the pain for Danson, just as she still feels the tight pull of the scar on her finger from a childhood injury. She's not spoken to Danson in almost twenty years, and it's more a tug than a gaping wound, but the hurt lives in her. Qasim is an ever-present memory. He flits in and out of her life with some regularity. The scales accumulate, like a lizard's, and slough off, but the new scales contain the cellular structure of the ones lost many years before.

"Dianna, are you there?" Qasim's voice jolts her again.

"Yes, Qasim, I'm here," she answers, sipping her coffee.

"Do you have other plans?"

"No." Silence again.

"I wish you'd reconsider," he says.

A chill ripples all the way to her toes. "I'm no longer a babe in the woods, Qasim."

"I know that, you old lady." He chuckles. "I'm the babe in the woods when it comes to you."

"Don't give me that," she says, but she hears the smile in her voice. "Peter Pan, perhaps, but no baby."

"We've both grown. We've grown together." His voice trembles. "Don't tell me you don't have feelings for me."

"Feelings don't make reality."

"Please, Dianna. Just coffee. I want to see your face. I have something to share with you. In person."

"Where are you now?"

"Tariq's apartment."

Why doesn't he want to be alone with her? "And is your girlfriend here yet?" She should have called her partner.

"She's not here."

"You're asking too much of me," she hears herself say. "I need all of you."

"We've both been asked to give more than most souls could take," he cuts through the heaviness that extends between them. "I wish I could have given you everything, but I had my family, my country . . . Dianna, don't give up on me now."

"All right then, coffee." She sits on the stool in the corner of her kitchen for fear her legs will give way.

"Good. I've never been up the Empire State Building. Do you want to meet there?"

Dianna rolls her eyes. "Please, Qasim, you've got to be kidding. That's hokey, even for you."

"What do you mean?" he asks. "You don't want to?" His voice has genuine incredulity.

She backtracks. She has forgotten how few movies and plays he sees. Work, always work. "It's just the oldest, most cliched movie plot in the world."

"Oh. Well then . . . Maybe . . ."

She interrupts. "No, no. If that's what you want. Let's just not stand in line to go up. You'll freeze."

"It's just near the place I have my meeting. How long does one need to stand in line?"

"An hour or two, on a winter day."

"Well, I can manage that if I'm in line with you."

Dianna groans. Will this man never grow up? Why does he still dust off such schoolboy lines?

"Should we say tomorrow around 3:00 p.m. or 4:00 p.m.? Can you get off work?" His voice has become gravelly. Dianna hears a siren sound on his end of the phone.

"Qasim, when did you get in?"

She hears his intake of breath. "Today."

"You must be exhausted," she says, and she is irritated at the softness in her voice and turns it formal. "Yes, I'm sure that's possible. Tomorrow at 3:00 p.m. The corner of 5th and West 42nd. That's the New York Public Library. We can at least spot one another there; then we'll walk the few blocks there together."

"Then we'll stand in line and go to the top?" His voice becomes almost a whisper now. "Promise?"

"Not the kind of 'top' you're expecting," she chides, but she hangs up with a small smile tugging her cheeks upward.

CHAPTER TWENTY-NINE: EMPIRES

March 1, 1994
New York City

The tension surges through her muscles even before she catches sight of him. There he is, in his double-vested navy overcoat. She can see him shivering from a block away, his hands stuffed like ostrich heads as far down in his pockets as they can go. From a distance, he looks just like he did that freezing night outside the pizza joint in 1981, only a bit more stooped from too much time at his desk. All the discourse she'd practiced that morning fades away. All that is left is a raw feeling. She is trembling, too, and not from the cold.

At first, they look at the sidewalk instead of each other. She raises her eyes to his face first. His face is gaunt and rigid. Is he still in pain? When he finally looks up to meet her gaze, his eyes are cloudy with tears, yet they bore into hers like a harbor's beacon through a storm, both welcome and warning. She felt closer to him on the telephone before. Here and now, their reserve seems to span like a world between them. She's not going to ask him what happened in public. That's probably why he wanted to meet her here, to feel her out. Or maybe he's going to tell her that he's made up his mind to stay with . . . she couldn't say her name. She's an innocent woman, just like Dianna had been, but the thought of Qasim touching her . . . Her heart spins.

Then he offers a hand, a bridge, an olive branch. She knows how painful it is for him to make the first move, to remove the hand from the warmth of his familiar pocket. She grasps his hand in her own, but she can feel no body heat because of their gloves. She leans over and gives him a perfunctory hug. His lips search for hers, and she gives them to him, but only for a slight moment. Still, the electricity stings as his skin brushes hers.

"How is work?" she asks as they begin walking. "How's your health?" She is vaguely aware of people coming and going on either side, brushing, pushing against them. She wants to create an envelope that protects them from the jostling crowd, even if it is with verbal banter. They've always been protective of each other, and he still looks ill.

"I don't have much hope, you know," is all he says. His eyes return to the ground.

"Hope?" Dianna wonders whether he means for his work or for something bigger.

"I've worked all my life for peace," he says. "I don't have much hope for it in my lifetime. Whenever we make a small educational or economic advance, forces take back the ground we've gained. Sometimes it's in my region, sometimes another part of the world. It seems the entire globe is against peace in the Middle East. Oh yes, they give peace their words, but their actions speak conflict."

"It's more complicated than that," Dianna interjects.

Qasim frowns. "Is it? Is it, my Dianna?"

"Every push and pull creates motion, and motion changes things, no matter how gradual. It may not be the change we hope for, but by doing our part, we at least are pushing the pendulum toward peace." She wonders which of their assumptions is correct, pondering this new despair from a man who was once full of hope. "Perhaps you are right. But it isn't right to give up. You were meant to be doing what you are doing. For the next generation, or the generation after that."

"Oh, no, I haven't given up." He laughs, throwing up his hands like he's throwing his worries to the sky. "On Peace. Or Love." He gives her a peck on both cheeks, then holds her face between his gloved hands. "I just am a bit more realistic these days."

"That's funny." She laughs with him, wondering at their laughter, which almost feels out of control. "I think I'm becoming less a realist, more heart-driven. Otherwise, I wouldn't be here in frigid weather holding your hand. Maybe there's something we haven't thought of, though—something more 'realistic'—that might bring things closer to resolution."

"You think on it, Dianna," he says and takes her hand and squeezes it. "You know, you may have the answers."

She smiles a real smile at him. "I will." Was Qasim actually listening to her these days?

They take the remaining block and a half with a fast clip, and he pulls her into the line that snakes toward the tall doors of the second tallest building in New York. How cold it will be on top; the wind already blows hard here on the ground. He won't want to stay outside on top long.

"Yet, I, for one, am going to take a desk job for a while," he continues. "I need a reprieve. All this traveling, all these sleepless nights. I need a break for a while. Maybe retirement in the next few years."

"You? Retirement?"

He blushes. "It's been twenty-five years of near nonstop air travel. Maybe just a sabbatical. Maybe then I'll go back."

"Yes, I've had my break," Dianna says. "I'm ready to go out again and try something new. I think working with women may be the way to go. They have so much invested in peace."

"Even they . . . even they are taking up arms." Qasim sighs, and he squeezes her hand again. "Now is the time to reach them before they become another large faction to contend with. They have spent lifetimes trying to make ends meet, to keep their families going, but most have failed. They have lost too many loved ones. Would you not want to kill the ones who had killed your child?"

They inch up in the line. Khalil's face surfaces in her mind's eye—as real as it was in Africa—and she shudders. The sun comes out from behind the tall buildings and shines in their faces. She takes out her sunglasses, and Qasim shields his eyes with his hand. He shivers as if in response to her.

"I don't know the answer to that question," she says. "I have no children. I do know that loving a child and losing that child, even though he carried not one drop of my own blood, even though we knew each other only a short time, devastated me. I know I wanted revenge, although not to the point of murder." She looks down, then up again, searching for words, making sure she speaks the truth. "I don't know the answer," she repeats.

"Nor do I," Qasim says. "Yet I have the feeling that the hourglass is almost empty, out of time to heal things, at least for a long time to come. All this new generation knows is death."

"I agree," Dianna says. "That's why I'm going to accept if they offer me a position on the West Bank."

Qasim's eyes widen. His head moves in a familiar but forgotten gesture: partly nod, partly shake of disapproval. She wonders at his alarm. After all, he has just returned from the Middle East. She wants him to see her as she is now, in the present, perhaps more flawed, but also with wisdom and strength to meet the challenge.

His words today suggested he was seeing her as more of an equal. Why is he dismissing her now? "I'm up to it, Qasim," she says. "You don't know the half of my time in Africa."

"I'm quite sure I don't want to know," he says. "I worry enough as it is about you."

It stirs her that he thought much about her when he wasn't within local dialing distance. If he was in Nairobi, he pulled on his Superman cape to rescue Lois Lane. But she'd always surmised he compartmentalized his life, that she was in a box or on a shelf when he wasn't standing beside her.

"I keep thinking of you, sitting in my chair, looking at my rug, our first day together," he says. "And I become terrified for you—and angry at your risk-taking."

She pulls her hand away. "You have no right . . ."

"You are correct, my dear," he says. "I have no right to worry about you. I have no right to fear for your safety. I have no right to care about you. Yet they could lay forth a thousand laws, construct a million obstacles, and it wouldn't stop me from caring, from loving you."

Why must he say such things? If he's with another woman? She won't ask him in public, though.

"Nor I," she says, and she puts her hand back in his. Love can be likened to war. They both can pick up a life and hurl it, over and over, against the rocks. The love can be trusted, but that is all. Because their lives have been focused on, sometimes emotionally ravaged by, war. "We've not been separated by oceans, but by war." She hopes he's heard her. A circling helicopter drowns out her voice.

He has heard. "The only reason we ever met is because war drove me here, Dianna."

How did war games in the Book of Love compare with the real cost of young lives lost in battle? All those young boys lay buried off Omaha Beach. All those survivors who had to salvage lives, alone, after the Holocaust. All those Vietnam vets with P.T.S.D. All those homeless people in uninhabitable camps.

They should stop arguing. She takes his hand, removes the glove, holds his hand close, which now has a few age spots dotted here and there. She holds it up against the sun, examining it. Then she takes it to her mouth and covers it with kisses. They have this moment, and love engulfs her.

"Touch is how we truly know things," Qasim says, soft and low. "Can you feel how I feel about you?" He looks down at the ground, his eyes scanning the pavement, back and forth, back and forth. "Dianna?" he asks, and his voice is choked.

"I feel it," she says and wonders how she ever doubted his feelings. People in line begin to advance toward the tall building, and the jostling becomes more pronounced. She puts his hand back down, and he puts his glove back on.

Dianna glances at her watch. "It's already been an hour," she remarks. "We're almost to the door."

"See? Not so bad." He grins and grabs her hand and sticks it in his pocket with his.

She has many questions as she stands there watching the wind whip through his graying hair, shoving it first to one side, then the other. She'd like to hear it all, just once, for the record. Perhaps they could each come to some sort of peace equal to their love. Yet where to start?

There he stands, buffeted by the breeze, eyes wide, foot tapping, humming some tune in his off-key *sotto voce*.

"How did you happen to be there, that night we met?" she decides to ask. She moves in closer, readying herself for any counterattack, all the same wondering at her reason for needing to know after all these years. The crowd begins to flood in an erratic zig-zag as they close in on the door. Dianna sticks her elbows out in her New York dare-to-get-in-front-of-me stance.

Then she knows the only two questions that really ever mattered. Did you always love me? Will you still, forever?

So she begins, "How . . ." But she only gets the first three words out. Ironic, she thinks as the interruption ensues, ironic how the moment of truth between two adversaries or two lovers is usually interrupted by an outside echo of their conflict. So that they might never arrive at the answer to the question.

A man in a Mets cap passes her, a grimace on his face. "They're closing the building. Might as well throw in the towel," he announces to all within earshot. "There's some crazy Palestinian on the Brooklyn Bridge shooting people."

Dianna looks sideways at Qasim. His face blanches. "Do they—do they know . . ." he stutters.

"Just some crazy guy," the other man answers. "Call it a day and go have lunch." He throws his hands up in the air. "I give up. Can't a tourist do anything in this damned city? I couldn't get into the Statue of Liberty yesterday either!"

Qasim's eyes shift from side to side. He looks like some cornered animal. Dianna looks around at the crowd. She can feel a few eyes piercing through her to gawk at Qasim. A few families move away from them. They are doing the same thing to a Hispanic couple a few spaces away from them in line. Will these people become afraid and attack them? She's seen it happen at home in the South, where fear spurred violence, on both sides.

"Let's go," Dianna says and puts her arm around him. She leads him out of the crowd as sirens sound in the distance. They retrace their steps, back toward the library, upsetting flocks of pigeons with their quickening gait. They stop in a little diner, and Dianna orders them both hot tea.

Qasim sits with his arms crossed at a table in the corner, his back to the windows. His teeth chatter until he takes the first sip.

"You didn't miss anything except a lot of wind," Dianna quips.

"Give me the top of the Eiffel Tower any day." Her voice trails off when he doesn't respond.

He sips, puts the cup down, picks the cup up, sips again for a long time.

Dianna puts her hand on his arm. "Are you alright, Qasim?"

"Of course, of course," he says. "I'll be fine. I'm just a bit cold." Yet his face remains pale and grave.

She doesn't know what else to say. She's flustered herself but hiding it for his sake. She looks around at the customers, who probably haven't heard the news yet. Sirens are not a rare sound in this metropolis. They sound like background noise.

"It's getting worse everywhere," Qasim says in a low rasp. "There's not a place that's not touched by this."

"Who's to say if it's terrorism, though," Dianna says.

"Why do Americans have to have a term for everything?" Qasim's voice rises. "A human being, a loaded gun. What does it matter if you call it murder, or manslaughter, or terrorism, or war, or desperation? I just pray he didn't kill anyone." He puts his face in his hands and rubs his eyes until she is afraid he will hurt himself.

"Come on back to my place," she says in a voice she hopes is more soothing than unsettled. "Come on. You can have a drink and lie down and rest a while."

He does not acknowledge her offer. He simply gets up and puts his gloves back on. Then he slams his hand down on the table. People look startled. They're not far from the attack. She needs to protect him.

"Do they think we are all animals?" His eyes dart from face to face. "We were so close, so close to peace. Yet all we get is reprieve. Lack of war is not peace."

If ever she loved him, it is in this moment. She's never seen how people might treat him, how they may have treated him here in her homeland. She's been treated the same way sometimes in Africa, even here, by men. Always on the defensive. It leaves a wound, a scar, and the scar tissue makes you tough, but poised for the worst to happen.

"Of course not," she answers. "No one who knows, let alone cares, about a Muslim could ever think that."

He looks near tears, and that's the last thing they want, to draw attention. "Come on. Come with me."

They walk the twenty-five blocks to her apartment. Traffic is snarled for miles.

•   •   •

The walk takes a long time, and he becomes more peaceful with each step. Right now, she'd follow him anywhere, but instead, she's leading him. Horns bleat, and the cacophony of idling motors and harried shouts fill the air as it becomes colder. The sun has disappeared behind the winter clouds. She keeps her arm around him, and he eventually wraps his arm around her shoulder, which causes them to advance in a syncopated pattern. Her stride no longer meets his, if it ever did.

He stops at one point and picks up a stone. "This is beautiful," he says, enunciating each syllable. The last sunlight glistens on the stone, a pink quartz, flat and clear, out of place in this place of dirt and gravel. "I want you to have it." He deposits the stone in her pocket. She does not protest. The stone is a survivor, from some time before this city rose around it. Time has smoothed its surface but has not dulled its beauty. They continue.

When they get to the apartment, they remove their shoes and sit on the new green angular couch. Dianna picks Qasim's feet up and forces him to lie down. She pours him a drink. He naps while she puts milk into the microwave to warm it for her cocoa. She picks up both drinks and sits beside him to drink hers. She pulls his feet into her lap as he used to do with hers. She watches his chest rise and fall, thankful he's still alive. The warm drink soaks into the chill in her body, and she almost dozes, but Qasim stirs and mutters. The creases on his brow become like small ravines. He is having a bad dream. She holds his hand, and he calms.

She wants this moment, so devoid of their usual defensive maneuvers, to continue. She puts her head down next to his and feels his breath on her hair. She gets her scissors, cuts a lock of her hair, and stuffs it in his overcoat pocket. She caresses his hair, thinning in places where it used to be lush, cuts a lock of his, goes to her bedroom, and places it in the center of her box. In some form, at least, they'll always be together. She'll have a memory. War or no war. She goes back and crouches next to him, her head next to his again. She measures her breath against his, in and out. "I love you, too," she says, and her throat catches. There, she's finally said it, but she's said it so low she doubts he heard it even in his dreams. She sleeps.

● ● ●

The cocoa is cold with skin on top when they wake. She warms up the cocoa, and Qasim sits up when she returns. He is holding a ring box.

"You should have this, even if you decide against me," he says. "I wanted to do it someplace special, but I suppose your home is as special as some silly landmark."

She stands very still. A ring. He gets up, puts the box in her hand, and she opens it.

The ring is not the one she expected. She thought it might be bold and beautiful, but this is feminine and delicate. It looks like a family heirloom. It's a stone she's never seen before.

"It's beautiful!"

"Like you," he answers. "Delicate like you as well," he says, eyeing her face for a reaction.

"My brothers took all three of my mother's rings," he continues. "They did not save me any for marriage, and it didn't matter to me at the time. My former wife had her own jewelry that she preferred. Now, though . . ." He runs his finger along her chin. "I wish I had something of my mother's to give you . . . Though this one suits you better. I went back to get it for you."

"Thank you," she says, wondering where the ring came from, wondering if this is an engagement ring. So like him to be oblique about a moment involving a ring. "You purchased it from a jeweler in Europe then, one who stocks your family's jewelry boxes?"

"No," he says. "It is from a trip to the Middle East when we were together—before. I saw it in a vitrine at a jeweler called Khoury. It was sitting next to a barrette, and I couldn't decide between them. I'm happy I chose the ring because," he motions to her shoulders, "you cut your hair."

"I cut it when I went to Africa," she interjects.

He nods. "I always thought I'd buy you an emerald to match the green onyx of your university ring, but this one spoke to me. The store had just closed, but I returned to retrieve it the next day. I almost missed my plane."

She takes it out of the box, her mouth forming a perfect O. Then she hesitates because she has no idea which hand to place it on. Does he mean for it to be some sort of commitment? Engagement? Surely, he didn't mean to marry her way back then—

He steps towards her, places the ring on her left hand, and seals the gift with a long kiss. "It's not to replace your beautiful ring, Dianna," he says. "It's an addition. I've cut ties. I am a free man now. I'd like to marry you, but I await your word."

Dianna cannot resist what comes next. She may never be able to resist him again.

CHAPTER THIRTY: OUTSIDE INFLUENCE

May 1994
New York City

She has spent much of her life waiting, but this wait is the worst. He's made up his mind; now they're waiting for herself to be sure. It's time to have a dinner party, a night of female companionship. They've stopped offering advice unless asked, but she'll ask now. She wants confirmation of what her heart chants. The chant drowns out common sense, makes her mind absent. She left her driver's ID somewhere. Hasn't yet gotten another one. Isn't sure she even needs a U.S. driver's license. The old Dianna would never have lost it. But this Dianna lives more in the clouds than on the ground.

She chooses a week when Leah is liable to be around.

Sophia arrives first, gives her a warm embrace, and hands her a bottle of Scotch. "I figured you needed to stock up." She winks.

Leah gets there last with Thing One in one arm and Thing Two perched on her shoulders. "Sorry, I had to take a shower from my workout." When will Leah learn to be on time?

Aisha arrives, wafting a dish that smells of spices. "What's that?" Dianna asks, taking the dish into the kitchen.

"Spinach with peanut butter. You never had it?"

"No, I was on bread, water, and Meals Ready-To-Eat much of the time."

Aisha clicks her tongue. "I should teach you to cook. You can't only feed a donkey when you want to ride it."

Dianna chuckles at her proverb. "I was their donkey, eh? Thanks, but you'll only have so much time. We should begin the meal so you can stay for it. Where are the children?"

"Downstairs with my eldest. I'll probably fetch them for dessert. I'm looking forward to some storytelling and laughter."

"Me too!"

She serves Sophia and Leah a Kir cocktail and hands a berry-flavored club soda to Aisha.

"To girl power!" Leah toasts.

"How was your last mission, Leah?" Sophia asks.

"I'm not sure I saw much to talk about. I was holed up in a hotel for two weeks. Landmines everywhere."

"Where were you again?" Aisha asks.

"Zimbabwe, believe it or not. They're one of the better ones, though. I think Angola has the most landmines at the moment. Somebody needs to do something."

Sophia sniffs. "Tell that to their leaders. To our leaders."

"There's talk of a treaty."

"There are always talks."

"Yes, well, maybe a new leader will do something about it."

"Only if that is a woman, a mother," Aisha says.

"Probably true," Dianna says. "I'm thinking of going back, but this time a little differently. Maybe in a way I could do more to help."

"I thought you turned Addis down?"

"Yes, I'm not even sure I'd be looking for a paid job."

"What? You've just inherited from a long-lost relative?" Leah chuckles.

There's a round of applause and the clinking of stemware.

"Hate to let you down, but no. I'm thinking of joining Qasim."

Silence permeates every corner of the room.

"I take your hush means you don't approve?"

Sophia is the first to speak. "I'm just surprised, Dianna. I wish you well."

"But you don't feel it's the correct decision?"

"We shall miss you, Dianna," Aisha says, touching her heart. "But a woman and a man are meant to be together."

Leah looks shocked. "Together? When have they ever been together?"

Aisha's eyes blaze at Leah. "Always. Two hearts bound . . ."

"Come on, Aisha. They may be bound to love unrequited, but do you really think they could live together? Look at what he did to that other woman. What's her name? Larissa. He led her on then dumped her."

"We don't know that. He was alone. She was alone," Sophia says. "For nearly a decade."

"More than a decade," Dianna says. "Why should he have remained celibate? He said he'd almost given up on me. I had given up on him."

Aisha nods. "But the heart knows."

"Is he still with Larissa?"

"No, they broke up a while ago for all intents and purposes."

"Well, just make sure she knows that," Leah says.

"I will tell you what I told you long ago, Dianna, dear," Sophia adds. "Don't give up precious moments because of any risky future, which may never come to pass."

"Okay, guess I'm outvoted," Leah says. "I think any man who loved you would have taken your hand and said he'd do anything for you. I guess you're joining him? He's not coming here?"

"We're not sure yet," Dianna says. Guess it's too much to expect a unanimous vote.

Sophia gets up and hugs her. "You know you have our support, no matter what. Go to him. Let him come to you. What are you waiting for?"

"I'll miss you all, more than you know."

"Not any more than we'll miss you, Dianna." Leah beams at her. "Women stick together. We love you, lady friend. And besides, what will Thing One and Thing Two do without you?"

"I think they'll love you all the more, Leah."

"You've got my support even if my vote isn't solid, Dianna. Just be careful not to step on any mines," Leah says.

Aisha's daughter phones that the younger children are up, crying for their mother. Aisha can't stay after all. They hug farewell, and Aisha is gone, taking the treats with her.

The circle is broken, but she has her answer. A wish fulfilled.

CHAPTER THIRTY-ONE: RUN, WALK, STAND UP

June 1994
New York City

She's running every day, sometimes twice a day. Only now, it feels like she's running toward something–someone–instead of away from it. She goes down for her second run but checks her mail first. She finds a feather-light envelope. Is it from Mirembe or Qasim?

Dear Dianna,
Thank you so much for your attempts to get me into the New York offices. It was going to work, though I am still in California, and I am still a consultant only.

She says nothing about discrimination.

I was preparing to come your way when I received some bad news.

My family is in danger, and I must return to Sudan.

She doesn't say "home."

My father was shot, and my mother and siblings have nowhere to go. It was bad enough when you knew my area. It is getting worse every day. I have no time to waste.

Mirembe's father was a teacher. They must have attacked the school.

I wanted to express my gratitude for your hospitality when I visited and for your support over the past months. I will write again if I am able to return.
Best regards from your friend,
Mirembe

She goes upstairs and tries to call the place Mirembe was staying, but it's too late. She looks down. The letter is postmarked Nairobi.

There's not much she can do. She'll ask Aisha if she can think of any way to help, but that seems pointless from this far away. All she can do is pray. And thank God Khalil is not in Sudan.

● ● ●

Hours later, she's beside herself. The letter brought back a gnawing to the pit of her belly. It's triggered memories. That's what words can do. All the letters sent. Letters received. Letters unreceived. Letters unopened. Unanswered prayers.

She pulls on her shoes and knee brace and heads out. Her knee hurts, so she'll have to give it a rest. She can still walk.

Under her building's canopy, she comes to a dead halt. There's a protest outside, people marching and chanting. She almost turns around and goes back inside. Yet she recognizes the language the chant reverberates in. The signs, mostly in English, bear the same message.

"Never Again – Again!"

She falls into step with the march. "What's going on?"

A young man, tall and skinny, American, answers her. "We're marching against the murder in southern Sudan."

Dianna's heart skips. "Here, today?"

"Every day until we must stop."

The crowd is small but still a crowd, a rainbow of color and fashion, carrying signs in English but chanting in Arabic.

"Never Again – Again!"

She backtracks and knocks hard on Aisha's door. Aisha answers immediately, a puzzled look on her face.

"Come on, Aisha! They're marching! They're marching!" She pulls on Aisha's arm.

"What? I'm feeding the baby . . ."

"No, you've got to come."

"I need to get the other children from the neighbor's flat."

"Now, or we'll lose them."

Aisha frowns but complies. She changes the baby's training pants, grabs her stroller, and throws on a thin wrap—part cover, part baby carrier. "Marching for what?"

"For Southern Sudan. For the killing in Southern Sudan!"

Now Aisha's pace picks up. "Outside?"

"For the moment. Hurry! They may be gone. We can't see from here."

The tail end of the demonstration is just turning a corner a few blocks up. Dianna races toward the undulating line. Aisha hoists Ibrahim up and around her hip and run-walks to catch up. "Wait! I must put Ibrahim in his carriage."

Dianna halts and turns around. Just then, a woman with a sign rounds the other corner. "Have you seen . . . ?"

"The march?" Dianna asks. "Yes, come on!" By this time, Aisha has her son secured. They haul ass down the street and arrive short of breath at the end of the parade. The noise led them to it.

The baby looks bewildered and puts his thumb in his mouth. Dianna feels a pang of regret. She hopes she's been right in inviting them to the rally. It might get unsafe for a toddler. But Aisha looks determined now, as though she's got a reason to be there. As she does.

"Is this the first march for Southern Sudan?" she asks a nearby woman who seems to have the most authority in her group.

"Yes, but not the last."

"Did something occur to catalyze this protest?"

"Murder isn't enough of a reason?" The woman scowls at her. "It's happening every day. Now rape. Even on the border now. They all flee to Ethiopia, and they slaughter them on the way."

Dianna almost stops in shock. That's how bad it's gotten?

Then she sees the photos. One is of a woman, disemboweled with flies encircling her. Beside her is a tiny baby, a fetus, really. They must have torn it out. "Yes," the woman beside her tells her as if she's read her thoughts. "That baby was alive when they tore her out of her mother's womb. They slit its throat before it could utter its first cry."

The signs and posters fill the space amid the continuous chanting. She's shocked at some of the wording:

"GENOCIDE"

"How Soon We Forget!"

"Two million and counting"

"Stop the Murder in Schools and Hospitals"

And one makes her heart stick in her throat:

"EDUCATION is my mother and father."

They march on.

She wishes she'd brought water in her rush. Ibrahim has his bottle, but the two women begin to slow. Dianna's not even keeping up with Aisha.

"How far will you march?" she asks a young man to her right. Her mouth is parched, and sweat streams down the length of her body. The memories flood back.

"Until we drop."

"Have you marched a lot?"

"This is our third march, our first for Southern Sudan."

"And why now?"

He looks at her and shakes his head at her naïve question. "I escaped. My family did not. My tribe did not, for the most part. The people are farmers with landmines all over their fields. They've burned and pillaged and left my home in rubble, my land a desert. If not now, when?"

"How did you escape?" Aisha asks him. The baby is starting to fuss.

She hoists him up, and Dianna takes the stroller. "My father searched for food, a gun, anything that would help our family survive. They tied him to a tree and shot him. I found him like that, after they were on the move again."

"Who?" Aisha asks.

"We may never know. Our enemy."

"It was just on the verge of full-out war when I was there," Dianna tells him. "You could feel it. The air palpated with it."

The man's eyes widen. "I am Daniel," he says. "Where were you?"

"Piecewood Camp."

Daniel's eyes narrow now. "With Biel and his lot?"

"Yes." Dianna wants to deny it, but why should she?

"He is not helping matters." Daniel spits on the ground.

"How did you leave?" Aisha's voice is calm, but her eyes are frantic. She must be wondering if her husband will be able to get out.

"My mother was killed by crocs. Many mothers died along the way. They'd pick us off like animals if we tried to cross the river into Ethiopia. We were mostly boys by that point. It took us three months to get to the border, and then that river . . ."

"Where were you?"

"At Panyido Refugee Camp, until that became violent, too. Then Kahuna Camp in Kenya. Talk about a desert."

"When's your next march?" Dianna asks him. "I'll be there."

"That makes two of us," Aisha says, just as a brick comes flying and hits her head.

The men all around surge toward the man who threw it while Dianna adjusts a wailing Ibrahim in his stroller and pulls the visor up as far as it can go. Aisha is rubbing her temple, but she's still standing.

"You've got a gash there," Dianna says. "We need to get you to a hospital."

"No hospital. I am just alright." Aisha shakes her head like she did the first night Dianna was going to call 911. "No hospital."

A fist fight has broken out. Sirens blare. "Let's go, Aisha, before Ibrahim gets hurt, too."

"No hospital." Aisha pauses. "No insure."

"No insurance. Okay. I'll have to call Tariq, then."

Aisha shakes her head again but not with such ferocity. She follows Dianna home, Ibrahim's baby blanket mopping the blood, which, thank God, is now only oozing from her scalp.

"Next time, Aisha, I'm going alone. For you. For me. For the people who've been murdered. And who will be murdered."

This time Aisha nods her assent.

• • •

Tariq arrives with a worried look. "Have you heard from my father?" he asks before she closes the door.

"No. Just that . . ." Dianna points to Aisha. Tariq clicks his tongue. "How did you do that?" he asks Aisha.

"Some asshole threw a brick at her," Dianna says. Aisha, who's been quenching her son's thirst, puts Ibrahim down.

"Where?"

"We were in a march for injustice."

Aisha's smile is wan, but it's still a smile. "Yes. Murder."

"What?!"

"Genocide in Southern Sudan," Dianna reveals.

"Women should not be out there doing that," Tariq says. He's sounding more like his father these days.

"Somebody has to."

"Well, it is not for women to do. Men should be out there."

"So few men left," Aisha says. "My husband will join them should he get here, in'shallah."

Tariq shaves a little hair off Aisha's scalp. "She needed stitches, but it's too late now. You should have taken her to the hospital."

"No hospital." Aisha's words have become a mantra, joining the earlier one in the street.

"I'll sterilize it, tape it, and bandage it. Take the gauze off tomorrow. Air will prevent more infection. Go buy some antibacterial ointment and make her use it three times a day."

"I have poultice," Aisha says.

Tariq rolls his eyes. "FDA-approved only," he tells her, shaking his finger for emphasis.

"FDA?" Aisha looks amused.

"Government-approved," Dianna explains.

Aisha says nothing more.

Tariq motions Dianna into the kitchen. "Make sure she lies down with her feet up for twenty-four hours. And check her pupils. If they dilate, give me another call."

"Don't worry. I'm glad it's the weekend. I can watch the children."

"You are a good friend to her," Tariq tells her. "Just be careful yourself."

"I will, Tariq."

His tilted head betrays his skepticism.

"I promise."

He shakes his head now. "I don't know who to worry about more, you or my father."

"We are two peas in a pod, aren't we?"

"Peas in a pod?"

"Similar but different."

He chuckles. "Yes. He couldn't have found a better partner in life. Just make sure you stay out of trouble."

"I promise. I can't vouch for him."

"Just stay alive so you'll see him again. It would crush him to lose you this time."

Dianna takes a step back. She never realized she mattered much to Tariq, or to anyone. Not really. She'd always wondered who would notice if her light was suddenly snuffed out. Something to live for. People to live for. A family.

"I'll stay safe. I'll find another way to speak for these women and children. But I can't stand by and let genocide happen without shouting about it."

"By the way, have you heard from my father?" He'd asked that question when he arrived.

"No, I thought you would have heard. Should we worry?"

"He's like this when he's on a mission. I think he has to do it to stay safe and sane. He, what's the word? He . . ."

"Compartmentalizes?"

"Yes, that's it. He spins a cocoon and only comes out when he's ready."

"Yes. And taking a caterpillar out of his cocoon kills it."

"You have a point. I'll not worry now."

She shakes his hand, but he gives her a hug.

"Take good care of Aisha," he says, kissing both her cheeks. "But take good care of yourself."

"I will, Tariq. Thank you."

After she closes the door behind him, she goes to prepare some dinner and get some more ice for Aisha. She's glad she'll be busy. She won't think about what Tariq said until she hears Qasim's voice again.

They watch the news that evening. "Look, that's the march! It's on every channel!" Dianna says. She looks for them amidst the brawl that followed but is relieved when she doesn't see them.

She does see an American man, a medical nurse. He, like herself, has spent time in Southern Sudan. The reporter is asking why he went there. "They are the strongest people I know, full of love and community. I can't end the conflict, but I can save one life," he says. "Who saves a life, saves the world. We all have a voice, and I'm using mine for them, the dead and the living."

"We need to do the same," she says to Aisha, who only stares at her. "Let me get you some pain reliever."

"No medicine."

She brings the rest of Aisha's children upstairs, and they pile into bed with her. Aisha sleeps on the couch, exactly where she's been sitting all day.

"Your husband will make it here, Aisha." Dianna pulls the sheet tight around Aisha's tall, thin body.

"Me, I am not so sure," Aisha says. Her eyes go to the ceiling, to Heaven. "In'shallah."

"In'shallah. We will find a way."

Dianna tosses and turns. She's got kids in her bed, is concerned about Aisha's husband, and is trying to figure out how to help refugees spilling over Sudan's borders.

But it's Qasim's face she finally dreams of in her hour of fitful sleep.

CHAPTER THIRTY-TWO: CONCOURSE

July 1994
New York City

"Hello, my dear. I found Khalil, or rather Jamal did, and he wants to see you."

She struggles to hear his voice. "Where are you calling from?"

"I am in Beirut by way of Budapest."

"Where is Khalil?"

"He is with his mother in Paris, but they are traveling to Mombasa next month. I told his mother we would meet them there, and I had to explain who you are and what you did for him. She was still distrustful of my intentions. She had no idea who I was, of course. For all she knew, I could have been lying."

"Did she agree to meet with you?"

"Finally, yes. If I brought you. Khalil was the one who convinced her."

263

"I am beyond joyful." Dianna paces around her office, her heart jumping out of her chest. But it is with happiness now instead of the dread she used to feel. A new future. And a chance to have Khalil and his mother in her life, or at least to say a proper farewell. Khalil was old enough now to understand what had happened. How she'd tried to protect him.

"Can you get here?" Qasim sounds as if she might run again.

"Of course . . . Qasim? I'm quitting my job. I was waiting for this call. I'm sure they wouldn't allow me a proper amount of time to get to him . . . and you."

"Truly? Truly my Dianna?"

"Truly. If you have had closure with Larissa."

"I have. Our final meeting went much better than expected. We had similar feelings, and in my absence, she found someone who fits her and her life. For now, at least."

This moment is surreal, more real than real. "And you are fine with it all?"

"More than fine. Dianna, you know I want to be with you, in whatever way you can be with me. Forever."

"Forever, Qasim."

"I have spoken to my family, and they want to meet you. Would you be able to accompany me to Beirut so I might introduce you after we see Khalil?"

"Of course! I will make arrangements today."

"Dianna, habibi, I send you my love for now."

"And I send my love to you, Qasim. Perhaps this long, painful limbo is over. Perhaps we have paid the price."

"We are better for it, you know."

"Yes. I realize that now. What we have learned, Qasim. From each other. About ourselves."

"We shall make a great team."

She hangs up the phone with a smile. It's not the kind of smile she used to have a decade ago, giddy and girly. That was romance. No, this smile is borne on the surety of unconditional love because only that kind of love is willing to pay the price.

She prepares her resignation, puts it in an envelope. Her boss is not usually even in his office. This time, he's there as if he's waiting for her. She hands him the envelope, packs her few belongings, and walks into her new life.

CHAPTER THIRTY-TWO:
ANCHORS AWAY

August 1994
New York City

Where is Leah? She doesn't want to order until she sees her. To Leah, this trip to Mombasa is just another adventure, but Qasim insisted Dianna not come alone. She's begun to agree with him. She's fortunate to have her friend travel with her to both countries, to act as a partner in her search for Khalil, to be an American witness to her nuptials in Beirut. She said "yes" over the phone, but they'll make it official in person.

Dianna and Qasim used to sit outside this cafe, watching the people come and go. She's come here because she knows she'll never be here again. She'll be with Qasim.

Will Lebanon compare to the pictures she has filed in her imagination? Will it pale in comparison to Qasim's descriptions?

She knows the first thing she wants to see: the mountains. And from the mountains, the aqua sea. And, of course, the famous cedars.

In that order. And then start all over again. From the beginning. But a new beginning.

That server over there was much younger the last time she saw him. Dianna is surprised to see he is still here. That other server over there is young and new. He sidles over to take her order, and she says she needs some more time. His nose is pierced, and his slick blonde hair needs a good shampoo. He smells like he cycled here.

There she is, in that cloakroom, bending over, her back to the door, taking off one sneaker, then the other, changing into her work pumps. She wears a pastel-striped blouse with ruffles at the neck and sleeves. Her long hair waves down her back, and the light plays through the blonde streaks as she bends at the waist, then straightens again. That is what Qasim must have seen when he entered in search of her.

A much younger Dianna feels Qasim's arms link around her waist, but she cannot see him. She turns, ready to slap the brazen man who would have the gall to clutch a stranger like that. She breaks into laughter when it's him. He laughs back. Their laughter fills the tiny space, which has become their own.

"What on earth are you doing in here?" He gives her a kiss. His lips are cool from the evening air.

"Changing my shoes." She hugs him, and they stand like that for a while. She takes in his scent—his cologne, and beyond it, the desert smell of his skin. She feels a bit embarrassed. She doesn't like him to see her in sneakers, but a mile is a long way to walk, even in slight heels.

"Oh, I forgot. You young women wear those athletic shoes to walk around town."

"You're on time!"

"So are you." They chuckle in conspiracy. She can't sidestep his wit, even when he is wiggling out of admitting his weaknesses. Qasim is almost always late. His eyes twinkle, and somehow in them, she can see the sun.

Back then, he was so private, withholding, that she thought he had a secret. When the secret had been that he loved her.

That despite all his troubles back home, he'd loved her. That he couldn't figure out a way for them to be together if he were to return home, where his troubles—and his son and his ancestors—lived. He stayed away, worked too hard, kept his silence at times, picked arguments because they couldn't have each other, at that point. She had her own troubles back home that prevented her from being the girl his parents would've approved of. Not to mention that he was Lebanese, and she American. That he was Muslim, and she, Christian. That he was older and traveled, and she had yet to leave the East Coast. That he was divorced. That he was headed for a political life . . . until he ran away, into her arms.

Today's sun, the sun of a new century, glints on the new waiter's nose ring. Dianna jumps. He is talking to her.

"Have you decided, ma'am?" He brushes his greasy hair back with one hand and takes a pencil out of his pocket, licks it with the tip of his tongue.

"Why don't you just bring me a club soda with lime? I haven't even looked at the menu. I'm waiting for someone."

She gazes up into the crystal blue sky, no clouds to be seen, moderate temperatures, a slight breeze. As good a day for flying as she's going to get.

She goes inside to touch up her make-up. The café's windows used to have red velvet curtains, mirrors lining the walls, and dark wooden tables with benches. Dark and smoke-filled. Now it's more of a café than a dance club. The mirrors are gone, probably shattered somewhere in some junkyard, and the walls are now a bright antique white with huge retro advertisements framed along each wall. The tables are less massive and a bleached blonde wood. Now, it is strictly a no-smoking establishment. What would Qasim think of it?

At least the pay phone is still there. She dials Leah's cell phone but gets no answer. Leah has a mobile phone now. She hasn't bothered because she knew she wasn't staying long. What was that new area code? She can still remember every single one of her childhood phone numbers. Back then, you didn't need an area code. Way back when, when she was a child, her grandmother's phone was still attached to a party line. That party line had prepared her for the humanitarian life, the life of the collective, of diplomacy, the life of scrutiny and observation.

Dianna rinses her hands and looks at her watch. It's already 1:00 p.m. She dials Leah's number again, then sits at an empty table toward the back of the restaurant, where she and Qasim used to sit, digging for another number to call in her too-full purse. Its contents spill in every direction.

She follows the spilled contents like breadcrumbs until she returns full circle to the empty table and, one by one, replaces them in her purse.

Until something catches her eye that matches her memories. There, there is something. Over in the corner, there is a shelf. It is shaped more like a fireplace mantle now. Funny how the changing management has kept the one thing that didn't fit in the room before and doesn't fit now.

Her fingers linger on some letters scratched into the tabletop. She traces them with her nail. She looks down at the scratches, trying to connect them, to make them into some sort of word. It's a signature! "Q." There is no way she could mistake the way that "Q" is made. It is Qasim's signature. It bled through his credit card slip and has somehow survived in this wood that has been refinished from dark, dingy, dull wood to bleached modern.

He'd looked around the room, back at the credit slip, and cleared his throat. "How much is the bill?" he'd asked.

He already needed reading glasses. How old would he have been? Early forties? He had asked her to add the tip.

"What? You want my half?" she'd teased. He hated to ask for favors. He hated for her to want to open the door for herself. He hated for her to take off her coat before he had a chance to come to her aid.

His mouth tightened, but then it dawned on him she was joking. "You're going to have to start to be my eyes," he says. "At least for the small print."

She traced two big numbers in the air: a four and a seven. "Forty-seven dollars and sixty-two cents," she chuckled.

"How much tip would that be?" He was the professor now. He knew how difficult it was for her to do percentages in her head.

She thought a moment, then blurted out, "Six dollars?"

"Not enough," he answered.

"Oh, Qasim, can you stop?" she said, and miraculously, he did. He took her finger and put it over his lips, at first, like a parent would shush a child, and then he ran her finger around his top lip, then around to his bottom lip.

"Let's go home," he said.

She rises from what she'll now always think of as "their" table to return outside. Home, where is home now? When was the last time she thought of a place as "home"? The echo of the memory of his voice, now, that is home. A home that has always been as far out of her reach as the houses she called home in her childhood. Beirut, even Beirut without Qasim, has beckoned her entire adult life. Because his stories made her fall in love with it.

Finally, Leah's here.

Leah waves big and boldly and shouts, "I am *so* sorry! You wouldn't believe the lines!" She's holding out the tickets.

"What time is the flight again?" Dianna looks down at the boarding pass. "The tickets say two hours in advance."

"Oh, that's just nonsense." Leah motions the server over. He pretends not to see her.

"But this is an international flight," Dianna says. Leah hasn't spent all those endless hours in Africa killing time for planes that never arrived. She flies nonstop at the government's expense. "And we have a connection to make in Paris."

"Don't worry, don't worry," Leah says. "My throat is completely parched. I haven't had a thing to eat or drink since breakfast. I will die of thirst if I don't have a glass of water this very second!" She waves at the server again.

"Ladies?" the server says.

"I need a bottle of water," Leah says, "with a glass, please. And make it clean, okay?" The waiter walks away. A car backfires, and they both jump.

"And the check!" Dianna adds.

"Broadway was completely blocked, so I got out of the taxi and took the subway, but then it stalled, and then I just got out and walked the rest of the way. I guess we could have picked up the tickets at the airport, but I wanted to get assigned seats. We're in business class, after all."

"We are?" Dianna has never flown in business class.

"Sure. Miles." Leah smiles.

"Thanks, sweetie," Dianna says. She forgets her panic and frustration.

"Bet it won't be the last you see of business class." Leah gives her a wink. "Mrs. el-Kafry."

• • •

They race to the boarding gate. They're on time. The plane is late. "Here—reading materials. I picked up the newspaper to read as I was standing in line."

Dianna picks it up and skims the front page. The Justice Department has secretly subpoenaed an AP reporter's phone records. A former CIA operative explains why American counterterrorism is a myth. Israeli troops are raiding the West Bank. China has reported an AIDS epidemic. Her eyes finally rest on an article on the stymied climate change talks. "I can't believe this reporting," she says to Leah. "This is not even half the story."

Leah rolls her eyes. "Well, they only have so much space, Dianna."

"Yes, but it's the same thing, over and over. And it's the same thing in the French papers. The Americans see adhering to it as a threat to capitalism, and the Europeans see modifying it as a threat to development. I'll bet the Beirut papers will have another slant."

"Spin," Leah says. "We know all about that, don't we?"

"Yes," Dianna replies. "But I think it goes beyond spin. Even the reporters can only see their little corner of the picture. How can we hope for any kind of compromise?"

"None of us can expect to know all the story," Leah says. "Look at you and Qasim. It's all about perspective. Yours. Others. You can't expect anyone to know your whole story. People will judge. People will talk."

"I don't give a damn." Dianna reads on, willing herself, muscle by muscle, to relax. She said it, and she means it, for now. The final boarding call sounds.

"Come on, let's go, girlfriend!" Leah taps her on the shoulder.

Dianna folds the newspaper into quarters and sticks it in her pocketbook. Leah picks up her briefcase, and off they go.

● ● ●

They land in Paris thirty minutes late, with only an hour to catch the connecting flight to Mombasa. They race to the part of the airport where they need to identify and claim their luggage and then sprint across to the other end of the airport. Dianna's breath comes in short jabs that stab the air. A sea of women veiled in black fill the boarding area.

"Where are all the men?" Leah whispers again. She digs in her purse and pulls out some mints. "Here. Want one?"

Dianna rolls a mint over her tongue until the taste of spearmint floods her mouth and nose.

"What did I do with my ticket?" Leah asks. "Oh my God, I think I left it on the last plane."

"No, you didn't," Dianna answers, and she starts digging in Leah's carry-on. She pulls out her sleeping mask, ear plugs, a chewed-up paperback, and contact lens equipment. She reaches into the bottom and pulls out the ticket, along with a boarding pass. "Voila!"

Just as they get their boarding passes checked and seats assigned, the first rows begin to be called to board. The early morning sun hits Dianna's head, and she yawns.

"I just want to wash my face." Leah rubs her hand across her cheek, and it comes off coated with a make-up film.

"Stay here, Leah. You should be able to do that in a few hours." Dianna notices a woman staring at them from the row of seats across them. She must be African. She has a small boy in a stroller and is pushing him back and forth to quiet him. Her efforts seem for naught. Dianna smiles. Khalil would flit from rock to rock, never still. The little boy waves at Dianna, and Dianna waves back. His mother's eyes sparkle in acknowledgment as Dianna nods to her.

The loudspeaker lists their row. When they try to board, the flight attendant tells Dianna she has one too many bags to carry on. "*Désolée*," she apologizes. "We are fully booked."

The woman with the sparkling almond eyes intervenes from behind her. "Don't worry. You can take my overhead space." She hands the flight attendant a leather Gucci bag. "I only need my diaper bag during the flight." Her eyes smile at Dianna.

The cabin is full of cigarette smoke. Dianna coughs in recollection. She's in Europe now, where people find a way to smoke. The young African woman sits two seats behind them, and she begins to feed her toddler, who drifts off to sleep.

A man with a meticulously trimmed beard meets her eye. She stiffens as she feels his gaze scan her body from top to toe. She uncrosses her legs and leans back, searching for something to divert her attention. She looks over at Leah, who's dozing. She pulls out the wrinkled newspaper.

"Attention passengers," comes a Kenyan accent over the speaker phone. "The captain has just informed me that we will not be pulling away from the gates as yet. We have a discrepancy in headcount."

Dianna rolls her eyes, flips the page, and folds it back into quarters.

A man walks into the plane carrying a briefcase. Dianna notices out of the corner of her eye that his attire is immaculate. She takes no more notice until he taps her on the arm.

When she looks up, she feels faint. Purple dots jiggle in front of her eyes. She places her index finger at that point where her ribs meet to form the beginning of a Y. She feels like she did after a car rear-ended her in Kenya some years ago, sending her flying into the steering wheel and breaking a rib. Takes a deep breath which, once expelled, means that nothing, not one thing, will ever be the same again. She blinks, and her sight, though blurred, returns.

It is Jamal. An older Jamal but looking much the same. "What are you doing here?" she asks, her voice like stone, and Leah rises as though she's prepared to order him to exit the plane.

"It is not what you think," Jamal replies. *How does he know what she's thinking?*

The air attendant walks up and tells Jamal he only has a few minutes before they begin checking seatbelts again.

"I do not have much time," he says. "You've not changed a bit. Believe me, I thought I'd never see you again. Yet Beirut has not changed either. Nothing has changed in all these years. And here we are again."

If this is Jamal's form of apology, it has not moved her. He had basically taken Qasim from her, had manipulated him, had all but threatened him, to return to Beirut to fulfill his, Jamal's, plans for his future. Yet that future had not arrived.

"It's you—You stopped the plane from taking off on time."

His smile confirms he has done just that. She despises him, his power.

"What do you want?" she asks, standing to meet his gaze head-on.

"I would love to say I am here to forbid you to come to Beirut, Dianna," Jamal says. "Yet those days have come and gone. I have no control over the Lebanese government any longer. I never had any control over Qasim. No—I am not here to keep you and he separated but to unite you. Qasim sent me. He asked me to give you this message." With that, he reaches into his jacket pocket and produces a white envelope.

The thud of her heart—that echo—signifies she is still alive. Yes, she remains here, on this plane, on this runway, and Qasim must be in Beirut. He might as well be in the ether or over the rainbow. Why is he not here to protect her?

She stirs, settles her bones. She opens the envelope, which bears no return address or postmark. All it says is, '*I need you now, Dianna. Please join me.*' She turns the envelope over, looking for something to tell her more. There isn't even a signature. She knows it must be from Qasim, though. It is his handwriting.

Will she go?

Her mind pounds, *No. No. No.*

Her heart sings, *Yes! Yes! Yes!*

"He is in Beirut?"

"Yes. You and your . . . companion must get off to change the second lap of the trip, though. I tried, but they need your passport and visa. Then join me on . . . my jet. I'll take you to Beirut." He hands her a stack of currency, which she gives back.

"Why can't I stop in Mombasa? Don't I have a day to see Khalil?" she asks Jamal.

"We should defer that," he says.

"What is wrong?"

"He did not confide that in me. I have done what he asked. I have told you all I know. I wish you well, my dear. You will need good fortune on your side, but I am here to take you to him." Jamal turns and deplanes.

Dianna sees alarm in Leah's eyes. She seizes Dianna's arm with a force that shakes it. "Dianna, can you hear me? Are you having trouble breathing?" Leah's red curls swim in and out of her vision. Leah rings the flight attendant's button, and Dianna vaguely hears her asking for some ice.

"Here, chew on these." Leah pushes the wet, frigid chips into

Dianna's mouth. At first, she gags, but as she chews on the ice, she begins to feel the cabin coming back into view.

Where is she? Ah yes, Paris. She feels a longing to get on the next U.S.-bound plane. She also harbors a desire to stay put, right here in this airplane, with that caring almond-eyed woman sending her warm rays of concern and Leah holding her hand. What she really wants is to go back, to that pizza place perhaps, or that jazz club, or Qasim's old house with the rugs that looked a different color from every side. But she can't go back.

The memories flood in. The night she met Qasim in that loud bar. The long waits when he was working late. The shock she felt at seeing him in Nairobi. The call from the hospital. What could be wrong now? Why would he urgently need her now?

The flight attendant comes back on the speaker. "Ladies and gentlemen, Mesdames et Messieurs," she announces. "You must take your seats or deplane. We have been cleared for take-off."

"Should I trust Jamal?" Dianna asks Leah.

"You learned to trust me again," Leah answers. "We all are different people than we were. Maybe Jamal is, too."

It's too late to run now. She gets up. She and Leah are on Jamal's plane bound for Beirut in half an hour.

CHAPTER THIRTY-THREE: HOME BASE

An Hour Later
De Gaulle Airport, Paris

The airplane itself seems to sigh as it disengages from the gate. It backs up, creaking with its weight. They taxi to the runway, and Dianna closes her eyes and grips her armrests. The flight is bumpier now. Still no clouds, but a strong headwind. New air attendants now speak in Arabic instead of English.

Two other women, swathed in black, and a man are passengers in Jamal's jet as well. The man offers her a bottle of water. "I'm afraid to fly myself when it gets bumpy," he says, his forehead crossed with concern for her. "Are you afraid of flying?"

"No," she says. "I used to be. Not any longer."

She sees Qasim the minute they make it past security. He's still behind a glass partition, like the night he was waving through the foggy car window in front of the Met. He's holding something in his other arm. Is his arm in a sling?

The arrival line stretches out a mile, and she tries to glimpse him again, but the partition prevents it. Another barrier.

Yet this time, the rest of her life awaits on the other side. It feels more vivid than life. For this is a place she always thought out of reach, a place that would need to be visited strictly in her dreams. How did such a tiny dot on the map become such a large part of her soul?

Because of one person. Because of love. Only a few more minutes. She's counting the seconds.

"I'm so tired I could drop," Leah says.

Dianna hasn't even noticed how far they've flown. She's full of adrenaline.

They get through the line at last. The immigration officer looks at them three times before stamping their passports. "Business or Pleasure?"

"Pleasure," Dianna assures him.

"How long will your stay be, and an address of your hotel?

Leah pulls out a slip of paper and hands it to the official. "Two weeks," she says. He nods and waves them on.

"What were you doing, saying that? We don't know," Dianna asks.

"It got us through, didn't it?"

"What address did you give them?"

"I asked the air attendant the best place to stay in Beirut while we were flying. She wrote down this address."

"Thank you. I hadn't thought."

"That's why I'm with you, Dianna. That's what friends are for."

When they round the corner, she rushes to embrace Qasim but stops herself, realizing they are in Beirut. People stare at them. His arm isn't broken. The white bundle he's holding is an infant, no more than a month old.

"Welcome to my country, my Dianna," Qasim says, his eyes glistening. "I had you come here because I wanted you to meet someone."

He reaches out and places the baby girl in her arms. Her brown eyes widen at the sight of Dianna, but she does not fuss. There is such wisdom in her eyes, wisdom born of pain. This baby, only a few weeks old, has witnessed too much. Dianna can tell. Yet this baby is full of light, like she's come from another world. She's a survivor.

"Dianna, meet Salaam," Qasim says, rubbing the baby's forehead with his finger. "But if they let us keep her, and you do not object, we can also call her Noor or Nora. She can have a string of names."

"Why do you have a baby?" Leah chimes in. "Is that what this is all about?"

"In a manner of speaking." Qasim deflects her question. "She was abandoned in a war-pocked building in the mountains. I was up driving, stopped to eat, and the restaurant managers had found her. They wanted to keep her, but they thought I might be more apt to . . . convince . . . the officials."

"Why you?"

"They thought that with my . . . pull . . ." His face reddens. "I had more of a chance."

"But why did you accept the . . . request, Qasim?" She searches his eyes for an answer. They bore into hers with a passion she's not seen before, from him, from anyone.

"She's abandoned, Dianna; you know what that feels like." He takes her hand and squeezes it.

"But they asked you to . . . Do you mean to keep her?"

"They say her parents were . . . in love." He pauses. "Like us."

He must mean Christian. Muslim. Unmarried.

"But how can you keep her? What about the law?"

"I am Muslim and from a prominent family."

"But how will we prove I am Muslim? We're not even . . . she lowers her voice to a whisper . . . legal yet."

"Let us take care of that today," he answers. "Leah is here as a witness. My family is here, eager to meet you. And as I said, Noor Salaam is believed to be . . ." He lowers his voice. "Of Christian and Muslim parentage. The light of peace. That's what her name means."

Leah leans over Noor Salaam now, beaming. "See? No need to worry!"

"But where is Khalil? Did you find Khalil?"

"That is a long story, I am afraid," Qasim says. "He is again with his mother, but he is not the same. He asked me to share this letter and a picture with you, though, until you meet again. He'll need a few months to . . . heal."

"But?"

"He is in his mother's hands again, Dianna. We must trust her. He should have never left her to join his father again."

Dianna finds a postcard and photos inside the envelope. The postcard says, "I am alive. I am safe. Please do not worry. I never forget you. Thank you for looking out for me."

She turns the photos, Polaroids, over. Yes, they are the ones she took that she gave him to keep, covered with mud and dust, and faded. She'd asked Jok to take them, and a cigarette bribe had sealed the deal.

He'd taken several and had liked the importance of holding the gadget. This was Khalil's favorite, and he'd sent it to her. They are outside her dwelling, Khalil in her lap, grinning, almost miming at the camera. The second one is Khalil, grinning wide, one of his front teeth missing, holding the bright blue copy of *The Cat in The Hat*. The third one takes her by surprise. It's the one she'd taken of Khalil's hand, when he hid behind the rock. Underneath, he's scrolled her name, the words "cat" and "rain." The words are encircled with a heart.

The last photo is of Khalil with his mother, older, more serious, but smiling. His mother smiles too, and her arm encircles his shoulders. "See? He is fine for now. We need to meet with my family. We have much to do. Shall we go?" Qasim takes her hand.

"Promise I'll see him again, meet his mother, Qasim."

"We shall both see them again, my dear," he says. "Together."

When younger, she'd imagined this moment as different. Her youth taught her that Cinderella stories weren't real, but she'd expected to walk up an aisle with a bouquet, in a church full of hope and expectation, with her friends and siblings watching on. Yet that fleeting moment would not have remained. The joy of this love, this love willing to pay the price, would. This love was what she really needed, more grounded, not from lack of adversity, but of love built on the back of struggle, first alone, to find her own heart, then together, to mesh with each other's heart, and now, perhaps with a child, to forge this love, for better or worse, into steel. It was that kind of unconditional love that set people free.

They walk out into the bright Beirut sunlight, and she sees the brown mountains rising in the distance. She has so many questions, but she's certain he'll answer them in the car. Does she want this child? Does he want this child? Will his parents accept their union? Can she make Beirut her home? She's unsure about the place, but her home is with Qasim.

They get to the car, and he grasps her hand. He gives her a long kiss for all to see.

A plane embossed with the cedar of Lebanon is taking off. It speeds forward between the white lines of the runway. It lurches forward, its engines churning steamy smoke. Then there is that momentary sequence that Dianna has always dreaded, that instant between earth and sky—when front wheels have left the ground, but rear wheels have not. For an instant, the plane hangs there, suspended. Then there's that echo, that *boum*, as both sets of wheels reach air.

She looks up at the mountains, twinkling in the sun, not a cloud in sight. They are on their way.

Dateline: South Sudan

Note: In the 1990s southern Sudan was part of Sudan. It has since gained its independence and is called South Sudan. Therefore, the author uses southern Sudan and not South Sudan when referring to the 1990s.

1899-1955 – Sudan, including South Sudan, is under joint British-Egyptian rule.

1956 – Sudan gains independence.

1962 – Civil war begins between North and South Sudan.

1969 – Group of Sudanese military officers led by Col. Jaafar Muhammad Numeiri seizes power.

1972 – Government concedes some autonomy for southern Sudan in a peace agreement signed in Addis Ababa.

1978 – Oil discovered in southern Sudan.

1983 – Second civil war begins. Fighting breaks out again between North and South Sudan, under leadership of John Garang's Sudanese People's Liberation Movement (SPLM) after Sudanese President Jaafar Numeiri abolishes South Sudan's autonomy.

1988 – Cease-fire agreement with the SPLM drafted, not implemented.

1989 – Military seizes power after government overthrown in a coup.

1991 – Skirmishes in South Sudan escalate.

April 10, 1993, Bor – International relief workers arrive in Yirol, finding only 30 people there alive. In Rumbek, they find three. In Kongor, more than 20,000 have died. There are few children and no cows or grain. This "silent" famine began due to floods, disease in cattle herds, and vicious fighting between rival tribal factions. General Omar al-Bashir is appointed president.

1995 – Egyptian President Mubarak blames Sudan for an assassination attempt on his life.

1998 – Oil exports begin. Al-Shifa Pharmaceuticals destroyed by U.S. missiles. American officials later acknowledge that there was no proof that the plant was manufacturing or storing nerve gas or linked to Osama Bin-Laden, a resident of Khartoum in the 1980s.

2001 – Sudanese Islamist leader Hassan Al-Turabi's party, the Popular National Congress, signs a memorandum of understanding with the southern rebel SPLM's armed wing, the Sudan People's Liberation Army (SPLA). Al-Turabi is arrested the next day.

2002 – Talks in Kenya lead to a breakthrough agreement between southern military leaders and Sudanese government, providing the South to seek self-determination over six years.

2003 – War and genocide begins in Darfur.

January 2005 – A Comprehensive Peace Agreement (CPA) ends civil war.

July 2005 – Former southern rebel leader John Garang is sworn in as first vice-president. A new Sudanese constitution giving the South a large degree of autonomy is signed.

August 2005 – South Sudanese leader John Garang is killed in a plane crash. He is succeeded by Salva Kiir Mayardiit.

October 2005 – Autonomous government is formed in South Sudan, in line with the 2005 peace deal. Former rebels dominate the administration.

2006 – Hundreds die in fighting in Malakal.

2008 – Tensions rise over clashes between an Arab militia and SPLM in the disputed oil-rich Abyei area on the north-south divide.

2009 – North and South Sudan say they accept ruling in The Hague that shrinks disputed Abyei region and places the major Heglig oil field in the north.

December 2009 – Leaders of North and South reach deal on terms of referendum for independence.

January 2011 – The people of South Sudan vote for full independence from Sudan, and the new country is named the Republic of South Sudan.

February 2011 – Clashes between the security forces and rebels in South Sudan's Jonglei state leave more than 100 dead.

May 2011 – North occupies disputed border region of Abyei.

June 2011 – Governments of north and south sign accord to demilitarize the disputed Abyei region and let in an Ethiopian peacekeeping force.

July 9, 2011 – Independence Day. A new state is born. A fragile peace evolves.

August 2011 – UN reports at least 600 people are killed in ethnic clashes in Jonglei state.

January 2012 – South Sudan declares a disaster in Jonglei State after some 100,000 flee clashes between rival ethnic groups.

April 2012 – South Sudan troops temporarily occupy the oil field and border town of Heglig before being repulsed. Sudanese warplanes raid the Bentiu area in South Sudan.

August 2012 – Some 200,000 refugees flee into South Sudan to escape fighting between Sudanese army and rebels in Sudan's southern border states.

September 2012 – The presidents of Sudan and South Sudan agree on trade, oil, and security deals after days of talks in Ethiopia.

March 2013 – After a bitter dispute, Sudan and South Sudan agree to resume pumping oil, withdraw troops, and create a demilitarized zone.

June 2013 – President Kiir dismisses Finance Minister Kosti Manibe and Cabinet Affairs Minister Deng Alor during a financial scandal.

July 2013 – President Kiir dismisses entire cabinet and Vice-President Riek Machar in a power struggle within the governing SPLM.

December 2013 – Civil war erupts as President Kiir accuses his former vice-president, Riek Machar, of plotting to overthrow him. Rebel factions seize control of several regional towns. Thousands are killed, and many more flee. Ugandan troops intervene.

January 2014 – A ceasefire is signed but broken several times. Fighting displaces more than a million people.

April 2014 – Pro-Machar forces sack the oil town of Bentiu, killing hundreds of civilians.

August 2014 – Peace talks in Ethiopia drag on for months as fighting continues.

April 2016 – Riek Machar finally returns to Juba and is sworn in as first vice-president in a new unity government and dismissed shortly after. He goes into exile.

November 2016 – UN fires Kenyan commander of its peacekeeping mission over the failure to protect civilians in Juba during July violence. Kenya withdraws its troops. Japanese peacekeepers arrive in South Sudan with a mandate to use force if necessary.

December 2016 – A UN commission on human rights concludes ethnic cleansing is underway.

February 2017 – A famine rages in South Sudan due to civil war and economic collapse.

May 2017 – President Kiir declares a ceasefire.

August 2017 – Refugees fleeing violence in South Sudan to Uganda passes the one million mark, according to the UN.

2018 – President Kiir signs power-sharing agreement with Riek Machar and other opposition groups in a bid to end the civil war.

2019 – Cabinet and regional governors asked to resign to end protests. Military topples President Bashir in a coup. A new government takes office under Prime Minister Hamdok as part of a power-sharing agreement between military, civilian, and protest groups.

South Sudan's story is complex and ongoing. For a fuller chronology of politics and conflict in Sudan and South Sudan, visit https://www.bbc.com/news/world-africa-14095300.

To view maps of Southern Sudan in the 1990s and present-day South Sudan, visit https://www.worldatlas.com/maps/south-sudan.

Dateline: Beirut

October 1990 – The Syrian air force attacks the Presidential Palace in Baabda, Lebanon, and President Michel Aoun flees, formally ending the civil war.

May 1991 – Lebanese-based militias (except Hezbollah) dissolve, paving the way for the Lebanese Armed Forces to rebuild.

July 1991 – Israeli shelling of southern Lebanon's towns and villages results in hundreds of civilian casualties and the flight of hundreds of thousands.

November 1991 – Hostage Terry Waite, who went to Beirut to negotiate the release of the other hostages there, is freed after nearly five years in captivity.

January 1992 – New elections take place for Lebanon's National Assembly. Syrian troops remain in Lebanon.

October 24, 1992 – New Prime Minister Rafiq al-Hariri, a wealthy Muslim Lebanese billionaire, names his government's key cabinet players.

November 23, 1992, Damascus – Syria declares it won't begin troop withdrawal from Lebanon until the Lebanese abolish their 49-year-old system of distributing government posts along religious (confessional) lines.

December 17, 1992 – Israel expels 413 Palestinians to Lebanon, and they receive little humanitarian assistance.

January 1993, Geneva – The International Committee of the Red Cross continues to be denied access to prison detainees in Lebanon.

February 22, 1993 – Lebanese Prime Minister Hariri meets with U.S. Secretary of State Warren Christopher to discuss the Middle East peace process.

June 1993 – Hezbollah launches rockets against an Israeli village. Israel vows to retaliate.

April 1996 – "Operation Grapes of Wrath," in which the Israelis bomb Hezbollah. U.N. base at Qana is hit, killing over 100 displaced civilians. Israel-Lebanon Monitoring Group, with members from

U.S., France, Israel, Lebanon, and Syria, set up to monitor truce.

May 2000 – After the rapid advance of Hezbollah forces, Israel withdraws its troops more than six weeks ahead of its July deadline.

2004 – Parliament extends President Emile Lahoud's term by three years. Political deadlock ends with the unexpected departure of Rafiq Hariri as prime minister.

February 2005 – Rafiq Hariri is killed by a car bomb. The attack sparks anti-Syrian rallies and the resignation of Prime Minister Jamal Karami's cabinet. Calls for Syria to withdraw its troops intensify. Assassinations of anti-Syrian figures become the norm.

June 2005 – Anti-Syrian alliance led by Saad Hariri, son of Rafiq Hariri, wins control of parliament, and Hariri ally Fouad Siniora becomes prime minister.

2006 – Israel attacks after Hezbollah kidnaps two Israeli soldiers. Civilian casualties are high, and the damage to civilian infrastructure wide-ranging in 34-day war. U.N. peacekeeping force and Lebanese forces deploy along the southern border.

2007 – More than 300 die in the siege of the Palestinian refugee camp Nahr al-Bared following clashes between Islamist militants and the military.

2008 v Parliament elects army chief Michel Suleiman as president, and he re-appoints Fouad Siniora as prime minister of a "unity government." Lebanon establishes diplomatic relations with Syria for first time since their independence in 1940s.

2009 – International court tries suspected killers of former Prime Minister Hariri in Hague. The pro-Western March 14 alliance wins parliamentary elections, and Saad Hariri forms unity government.

2011 – Government collapses after Hezbollah and allied ministers resign. Najib Mikati forms cabinet dominated by Hezbollah.

2012 – The Syrian conflict that began in March 2011 spills over into Lebanon. Security chief Wissam al-Hassan is killed in car bombing. The opposition blames Syria, resulting in several days of fighting. U.N. praises Lebanese families for having taken in more than a third of the 160,000 Syrian refugees who have streamed into the country.

March 2013 – Syrian warplanes and helicopters fire rockets into northern Lebanon, days after Damascus warns Beirut to stop militants crossing the border to fight Syrian government forces.

May 2013 – At least 10 people die in further sectarian clashes in Tripoli (Lebanon) between supporters and opponents of the Syrian regime. Hezbollah leader Hassan Nasrallah vows victory in Syria. European Union lists the military wing of Hezbollah as a terrorist organization.

August 2013 – Dozens of people are killed in bomb attacks at two mosques in Tripoli, the deadliest attacks since the civil war ended in 1990.

November-December 2013 – A suicide bombing outside Iranian embassy in Beirut kills at least 22 people. Hezbollah leader Hassan Nasrallah blames the Saudi intelligence services. Hezbollah accuses Israel of assassinating senior Hezbollah commander. Israel denies any involvement. Former Lebanese minister Mohamad Chatah — a Sunni Muslim and staunch critic of Syrian President Bashar al-Assad — is killed by a car bomb in Beirut.

2014 – Sunni Muslim politician Tammam Salam finally assembles new power-sharing cabinet following 10 months of talks. The number of Syrian refugees registered in Lebanon surpasses one million. One in every four people living in Lebanon is now a refugee from the Syrian conflict. President Suleiman ends his term of office, leaving a power vacuum.

2015 – Israel launches air strikes on Syrian side of the Golan, killing Hezbollah fighters and an Iranian general. Syrians face new restrictions to enter Lebanon. By summer, suicide bombings, allegedly by Syrian nationals, aggravate already strained relations between Lebanese citizens and Syrian refugees.

January 2020 – Protests against economic stagnation and corruption bring down the government of Saad Hariri, who is succeeded by the academic Hassan Diab.

August 2020 – After a massive chemical explosion in the Beirut port, Diab government quits. The explosion, declines in the value of the currency, and the impact of the Covid-19 lockdown result in rioting. The suffering continues.

For a thorough chronology of politics and conflicts in Lebanon, visit https://www.bbc.com/news/world-middle-east-14649284.

For a map of Lebanon, visit https://www.worldatlas.com/maps/lebanon.

More Resources

The following materials were essential to my research and served to refresh my memories.

My last trip to Lebanon was in 2006. I thank the Lebanese people for their hospitality and interviews.

Nonfiction

Next Time They'll Come to Count the Dead, Nick Turse, c. 2016
They Threw Fire on Us From the Sky, Ajak, Deng, & Bernstein, c. 2015
Emma's War, Deborah Scroggins, c. 2004
From Beirut to Jerusalem, Thomas L. Friedman, c. 2012
God Has Ninety-Nine Names, Judith Miller, c. 2011
Lebanon Rebuilt, Ayman Trawi, c. 2003
Pity the Nation, Robert Fisk, c. 1990

Fiction

The Map of Love, Ahdaf Soueif, c. 2011
White Masks, Elias Khoury, 2010
Story of Zahra, Hanan al-Shaykh, c. 1996

Periodicals

Lebanon's *Daily Star* Newspaper
"Lebanon, Little Bible Land in the Cross Fire of History," William S. Ellis, *National Geographic* Magazine, February 1970 issue

Documentaries

"Facing Sudan," Bruce David Janu, dir., 2007
"The Lost Boys of Sudan," Jon Shenk & Megan Mylan, dir., 2003

Acknowledgments

I wrote this novel in solitude, but I always felt such inspiration from other readers and writers around me, both the living and the dead. All views and my story are from my personal experience, but I want to commend those people whose stories inspired this one—from the Rwandan child with the machete in his skull who lived, to the Iowan mom who read my article about her son who died of AIDS at his funeral, to the displaced Somali who said, "thanks for sharing my— no our—story, with the world."

You'll find a bibliography of the print and online resources I used to expand on and verify my experience. I urge you to read or watch them. We still need to produce more awareness about Arab, African, and Muslim cultures.

Of course, a novel is a tapestry of an author's experience, perspective, travel, research, ancestry, and especially, imagination. I was born asking questions about war and peace, crime and punishment, due to my inquisitive temperament and to my family and its history. I took trips that transformed my view of the world. My work with the American Red Cross and, later, with the International Red Cross & Red Crescent created a perspective on these travels. Interaction with other cultures, most of whom were experiencing a trauma or disaster of some sort, if not running for their lives with no place to go, made it personal for me. The men I dated in my early 20s also have a bearing on this story, but so do my husband of almost four decades and the children we raised for half that time, both of whom were born on other continents.

I've been a journalist, a humanitarian worker, a novelist, a wife, and a mother over these years. I've written other novels before this one and gave up on them after a few rejections. This story would not let me go. I thank all who allowed me to bring it to them, to light in the world. My hope is it will bring healing to some of you.

First and foremost, my deepest gratitude goes to my agent Diane Nine without whom you would not be reading this book. To my publisher Sheri Williams, at TouchPoint Press, for taking both books in my *A Bridge Between Shores* series, and to the adept and incisive editor, Kimberly Coghlan, who polished my prose.

My colleagues at The National Geographic Society and the Red Cross and Red Crescent for allowing me to live a life to tell about.

Eternal appreciation and love to my husband Brian, my life partner, who encouraged me to be me, became what he calls "the trailing spouse" and an equal parent for our children.

The kind of unconditional love and gratitude that only a child can bring to my son Sean and my daughter Aimee Xiao Wei, for teaching me along the way that work is not everything and that our voices can do much to stop prejudice.

A shout out to my soul sisters and fellow writers Laura Schmidt Pizzarello and Stacey Vander Vennet Waller, who thought they could serve humanity better from the other side of the veil. I felt you holding my hand and rubbing my shoulders, and offering advice no matter where you are. Thank you, Stacey, for sticking around on Earth to celebrate my first novel's publication.

An equal shout out to my friends who've stuck with me here, writers, editors, and librarians all.

To those men I've loved and lost but carry in my heart, even if I had to bandage it for a while, I hope your dreams came true.

A special debt of gratitude for Nancy Kervin: editor extraordinaire and researcher and librarian to Senate and Congressional staff, who offered to do the final edit on my book. No one could have understood this book as much as you. No one else would have turned it around in such an impeccable state or on such a tight deadline.

Thanks to my writing group, We Seven (Donna Anderson, Tami Lewis Brown, Cynthia Campbell, Alice Covington, Candice Haaga, and Anne McNulty), and my online writing group members (Teri Case, Kim Hamilton, Mary Incontro, Lisa Sinicki, and Colleen Waterston.) You are my eyes and my strength. Thanks to Amanda Zieba for all those publicity tips, and to Dan Blank, who introduced all of us.

Appreciation also goes to this novel's many editors and advisors along the way: Jennie Nash, who told me a scene was fine the way I'd written it, Amy Sue Nathan, who was the tough editor I asked for and made me dig deep, Susan Breen, who gave me the best lessons on plotting and the market early on, and Michele Orwin, for your holistic approach and tips. You helped me out of the trees and got me over the forest. You are the best book coach ever!

To my two literary sisters who've shared my journey over the past five years: Johnnie Bernhard, the first author who truly believed in my characters as much as I did, and Kathleen M. Rodgers, one of the most selfless authors I know and a writer I admire and love being in the company of, especially on our Texas road trips.

For the authors who joined me on my "Story Hour," you inspire me more than you know.

To my intern Kailey Mullis, who kept going even amidst a death in her family, my assistant Tina Hilton, who keeps me humming online, John Perkins, who told me to keep on writing, Kiese Laymon, who realized Dianna was a runner and said I was almost finished, Jan Fuller, my birthday sister and fellow adoptive mother for your beautiful adoption story, which brought my novel to a conclusion.

To the taxi drivers I interviewed all over the world in the early 1990s, you may not remember me, but I remember you. Your story will not be forgotten.

And to my humanitarian colleagues, flung far around the globe, for our good times and laughs as we commiserated over our very real stories of sacrifice and hardship.

And final thanks go to my mother. I know you'd do anything to be in the audience of my readings and are, in spirit. I write for you before many. May you be a famous author in your next life. Until then, I hope I did you proud.

I leave you all with one word: Salaam.

About The Author

Kathryn Ramsperger's literary voice is rooted in the Southern tradition of storytelling and is informed by her world travels. She began her career writing for *The Roanoke Times, The National Geographic Society,* and Kiplinger publications and later managed publications for the Red Cross and Red Crescent in Geneva, Switzerland.

Writing from a global perspective, her themes are universal yet intensely personal and authentic.

A graduate of Hollins University (Roanoke, Va.), Kathryn studied under several esteemed authors. She received another degree in Publications Management as a post-graduate at George Washington University.

Winner of the Hollins University Fiction Award, Kathryn is also a finalist in the Faulkner-Wisdom literary competition. Her first novel, *The Shores of Our Souls,* won a Foreword Indies award for multicultural fiction and an America's Best Book Award. Readers' Favorite gave it 5 stars for social issues literature, and her novel is also an International Pulpwood Queens and Timber Guys Bonus Book of the Year. Her short stories have appeared in numerous journals, including *The MacGuffin* and *Willow Review.*

Kathryn interned for President Jimmy Carter, has dined with artists ranging from author Marita Golden to musician and writer Kinky Friedman, and has traveled to every continent except Antarctica and Australia. She's worked in Europe, Africa, and the Middle East. She currently lives in the DC suburbs. She and her husband have two adult children and a furry companion. When not writing, reading, broadcasting, and coaching, she's traveling and singing.

Find out more about Kathryn and read more of her stories at https://kathrynbrownramsperger.com.

To The Reader

Thank you for reading *A Thousand Flying Things*. I write for you. Please note that I wrote this book as a work of fiction, and while well-researched, it is about my characters and how war affected them, not facts and figures.

If you enjoyed my novel, I'd appreciate your review at Goodreads, Amazon, or your favorite store or social place to share online. As readers, we have more books than time, and I appreciate your choice to spend time with my characters. I'd love to hear from you. Connect with me via my website https://kathrynbrownramsperger.com, where you'll find a book club Q&A, a recipe e-book, character profiles, interviews, and other treats. You can also find me on Facebook at facebook.com/kathyramsperger or on Twitter and Instagram at @kathyramsperger.

CPSIA information can be obtained
at www.ICGtesting.com
Printed in the USA
LVHW030035120723
752230LV00037B/1216

9 781956 851649